SELECTED WORKS OF DAVID JONES

WORKS BY DAVID JONES

IN PARENTHESIS
THE ANATHEMATA
THE SLEEPING LORD AND OTHER FRAGMENTS
EPOCH AND ARTIST
THE DYING GAUL
THE ROMAN QUARRY

SELECTED WORKS OF DAVID JONES

from
In Parenthesis
The Anathemata
The Sleeping Lord

Edited by John Matthias

NATIONAL POETRY FOUNDATION
UNIVERSITY OF MAINE
ORONO, MAINE

CARDIFF
UNIVERSITY OF WALES PRESS

1992

All rights reserved. No part of this book may be reproduced, stored in a retrieval system, or transmitted, in any form or by any means, electronic, mechanical, photocopying, recording or otherwise, without permission from The National Poetry Foundation, University of Maine, Orono, Maine 04469-5752, U.S.A. and from the University of Wales Press, 6 Gwennyth Street, Cardiff, CF2 4YD, Wales

Published jointly by
The National Poetry Foundation
and
The University of Wales Press

Selection and introduction copyright © John Matthias 1992

This selection first published in 1980 by Faber and Faber Limited. Faber continues to control the copyright of *In Parenthesis*, *The Anathemata* and *The Sleeping Lord*.

Library of Congress Number: 92-80593
ISBN 0-943373-18-2 (cloth)
0-943373-19-0 (paper)

British Library Cataloguing-in-Publication Data
A catalogue record for this book is available from the British Library
ISBN 0-7083-1169-5

Printed in the U.S.A. by
Cushing-Malloy, Inc.

CONTENTS

PREFATORY NOTE by John Matthias   xi

INTRODUCTION by John Matthias   13

A, a, a, Domine Deus   31

FROM IN PARENTHESIS (1937)
- Part 3: Starlight order   35
- *From* Part 4: King Pellam's Launde   63
- *From* Part 7: The five unmistakable marks   73
- Notes to In Parenthesis   96

FROM THE ANATHEMATA (1952)
- *From* Preface to The Anathemata   115
- *From* I: Rite and Fore-Time   139
- II: Middle-Sea and Lear-Sea   149
- *From* VII: Mabinog's Liturgy   168
- Notes to The Anathemata   175

FROM THE SLEEPING LORD AND OTHER FRAGMENTS (1974)
- The Tribune's Visitation   197
- The Tutelar of the Place   211
- The Hunt   218
- *From* The Sleeping Lord   222
- Notes to The Sleeping Lord and other fragments   231

NOTE: Extracts from David Jones' books are in every case taken from the latest printing.

PREFATORY NOTE

The present selection of work by David Jones was initially published by Faber and Faber in 1980 as *Introducing David Jones*. At the conclusion of my introduction I expressed the hope that "this volume will extend considerably David Jones' readership and that new readers will be encouraged to begin for themselves a journey 'from the known to the unknown.' " This is still my hope. There is evidence that the Faber edition introduced the work of David Jones to many readers who had not previously encountered it at all; I trust that this new edition will find its way to even more such readers. While a great deal of very interesting critical work has been written about David Jones in the course of the last decade, it is important to stress that his writing is *not* just something for critics and scholars. *In Parenthesis* will be a shattering experience for *any* serious reader, while late monologues such as "The Tribune's Visitation" are, in their way, as accessible as the monologues of Browning. Having predicted in 1980 that Jones' future audience would come from both sides of the Atlantic, I would now notice the existence of a new readership, indeed a young readership, emerging as significantly in Australia (where the journal *Scripsi* has been leading the way) as in the United States and Canada. And of course in Britain and Ireland there has always been a loyal, if small, non-academic audience for his work which is surely still capable of being expanded. But I also acknowledged in my introduction "the considerable difficulty of some of Jones' finest texts," having in mind chiefly *The Anathemata*, and suggested where one might want to go to find help. That is the part of the introduction which is out of date.

In 1980, much of the best Jones criticism was still scattered in journals and smallish monographs. Today, the reader will be able to find most of the commentary which he requires in two books: Thomas Dilworth's *The Shape of Meaning in the Poetry of David Jones* (University of Toronto, 1989) and my own volume in the National Poetry Foundation's "Man and Poet" Series, *David Jones: Man and Poet* (1989). The latter contains essays on the visual art as well as the writings, together with reproductions of paintings, drawings, engravings and inscriptions; it also includes a fully annotated bibliography. In addition to these two books, I should mention what will continue to be the most useful biographical source until the publication of the biography on which Thomas Dilworth is working, René Hague's *Dai Greatcoat: A Self-Portrait of David Jones in His Letters* (Faber and Faber, 1980). The best text on the visual art is still, in my opinion, Paul Hills' catalogue for the 1981 Tate Gallery retrospective exhibit, *David Jones* (Tate Gallery, 1981). The best available reproductions of the visual art appear in two books by Nicolete Gray, *The Paintings of David Jones* (Lund Humphries, 1989) and *The Painted Inscriptions of David Jones* (Gordon Fraser Gallery, 1981).

These selected works should be read like the selected works of any major author: as an introduction to writings that will reward years of reading, not just weeks and days. Although originally intended for the general reader, the selection will also serve the needs of teachers and students of modern literature. David Jones' position in the canon of modernism would still appear to be insecure; but I have no doubt at all that he belongs among his canonized and only real peers: Yeats, Joyce, Eliot, Williams, and Pound.

John Matthias
January, 1992

INTRODUCTION
by John Matthias

There is a house in Cambridge called Kettle's Yard where, if you should want to look at several representative examples of David Jones' visual art, you can ring a bell and meet a Cambridge undergraduate who will show you, along with pieces by Gaudier-Brzeska, Ben Nicholson, Henry Moore and others, H. S. Ede's collection of Jones' woodcuts, drawings and water-colours, including the extraordinary *Vexilla Regis* of 1948 and the *Flowers of* 1950. The house is a visual, tactile equivalent for David Jones' accumulating written works. It is not exactly a gallery (are David Jones' writings exactly 'poems'?) but, as Mr Ede says in his introduction to the handlist of paintings, sculptures and drawings, 'a continuing way of life from these last fifty years, in which stray objects, stones, glass, pictures, sculpture, in light and in space, have been used to make manifest the underlying stability which more and more we need to recognize if we are not to be swamped by all that is so rapidly opening up before us'. These stones, pictures, sculptures and objects which he has assembled in his house are Ede's *anathemata*. He felt strongly, he says, a need 'to give to others these things which have been given to me; and to give in such a way that by placing and by a pervading atmosphere one thing will enhance another, making perhaps a coherent whole'. He has given his house and his collection to the university and now lives in a small cottage in Scotland. The handlist, set in Monotype Perpetua, a typeface designed by Eric Gill, has for a cover David Jones' inscription *Qui Per Incarnati*.... In this house and in this context, if anywhere, the author of *In*

Introduction

Parenthesis, *The Anathemata* and *The Sleeping Lord* does not appear to be, as the *Guardian*'s poetry critic had it a few years back, 'an eccentric figure on the periphery of English poetry'.

Which is why I went there to think about what I should say about this book. The temptation in writing these notes for new readers of David Jones, a temptation to which I think I ought to succumb, is to be wholly partisan, to acclaim—simply to point and praise. And why not, given my admiration for the work? Only because that kind of thing always has its strident side, and because stridency is pretty alien to David Jones' sensibility. As if one should stand outside Kettle's Yard and shout to passers-by: go inside and look at the *Vexilla Regis*! But what if no one does? And only because the artist may be considered an eccentric figure on the periphery of English painting? One of the great lessons we can derive from David Jones' career will come from the thought of his nearly infinite patience.

All of the pieces in this selection have been known to David Jones' admirers at least since the 1967 special issue of *Agenda* magazine in which most of the poems from what would become *The Sleeping Lord* appeared, along with reproductions of his visual work and essays by several hands on both his earlier books and what was then called his 'work in progress'. *In Parenthesis*, of course, has been in print since 1937, and *The Anathemata* since 1952. 'The Tribune's Visitation' first appeared in 1958, 'The Tutelar of the Place' in 1961, and 'The Hunt' in 1965. The poems, having been known for some time at least to a loyal band of readers, have occasioned useful commentaries. David Blamires' *David Jones: Artist and Writer* (Manchester, 1971; Toronto, 1972) is a fine book-length introduction both to the writings and the visual work, while excellent shorter studies are available in Kathleen Raine's *David Jones and the Actually Loved and Known* (Ipswich, 1978), Jeremy Hooker's *David Jones: An Exploratory Study* (London, 1975), and René Hague's *David Jones* (Cardiff, 1975) in the Writers of Wales series. *Poetry Wales* published a special David Jones number in 1972, *Agenda* produced a second Jones issue to coincide with the publication of

Introduction

The Sleeping Lord in 1974, and Roland Mathias edited papers delivered at the David Jones Weekend School at Aberystwyth in 1975 under the title *David Jones: Eight Essays on His Work as Writer and Artist* (Llandysul, Dyfed, 1976). More specialized are René Hague's invaluable *A Commentary on The Anathemata of David Jones* (Wellingborough, Northants, and Toronto, 1977), the recently published introductory guide to *The Anathemata* and *The Sleeping Lord* by Henry Summerfield (Victoria, B.C., 1979), and Thomas Dillworth's *The Liturgical Parenthesis of David Jones* (Ipswich, 1979).

I mention these publications for two reasons. I want to call attention to work done by the best critics of David Jones and at the same time acknowledge the considerable difficulty of many of Jones' finest texts and suggest where to go to find help. A good deal of help is provided in Jones' own notes and glosses, and still more in his collections of essays brought together under the titles *Epoch and Artist* and *The Dying Gaul*. The notes and essays, in fact, are an organic part of the corpus of his work. It is all one: *In Parenthesis*, *The Anathemata*, the *Vexilla Regis*, the late water-colour drawing *Trystan Ac Esyllt*, *Epoch and Artist*, *The Sleeping Lord*, the note on the Catuvellaunian King Cunobelinos and the note on the pronunciation of the Welsh word *gwaundir*—all the poems and essays, all the drawings, etchings, water-colours, inscriptions and notes—'part of a continuing way of life from these last fifty years'.

How does this continuing way of life touch ours? 'As far as I can see,' Jones writes in a letter to René Hague, ' "man-the-artist" and "man-the-priest" become increasingly, in a sense, Ishmaels, or men of a kind of diaspora, within our technological set-up.' Living in what Jones calls our 'megalopolitan twilight', it is not everyone who can say with Stuart Piggott, the archaeologist, that Jones' emotive referents are his own—'from Mesolithic to Mabinogion'. Much of our response to Jones, in fact, is conditioned by an encounter in his work with sheer *otherness*, things otherwise opaque made numinous by the craft of the maker. There is something in the quality of his wonderful inscriptions—two of which are included here—that extends to

Introduction

many of his texts. The later work in particular is not only richly allusive, but is studded with words like *trefydd* and *pentan*, *palasau* and *arglwyddi*, along with the more familiar Latin and Anglo-Saxon. In general, Jones would stress (he does so in his Preface to *The Anathemata*) the impossibility of achieving in English an identity of content and evocation for such words, before going on (as he does in a headnote to *The Sleeping Lord*) to consider their musical function, or a desire for a rich and dense texture, or a craftsman's determination to use a word as a *thing*, as an object to be moved here or there, to be seen in relationship to this or that. But his willingness so often to think out his music in terms of the nominative, of the-word-as-a-noun, produces a texture which is wonderfully knitted with the stuff of otherness: we want to run our finger over the page.

But, along with materials deriving from the 'unshared backgrounds' which Jones painstakingly opens up for us in his essays and notes—notes which are often themselves short essays and which he rightly insists are *not* pedantic, but 'only mere politeness'—are those deriving from certain backgrounds which he can still assume are shared by many readers, North American as well as British, and which, as the strange therapy of his language works against our amnesia, we begin to remember. In 'The Wall', one of the Roman poems from *The Sleeping Lord* not included here, there occurs this embroidery of sound:

     Did the empyreal fires
hallow the chosen womb
      to tabernacle founders of
      emporia?
Were the august conjoinings
      was the troia'd wandering
      achieved
did the sallow ducts of Luperca
      nourish the lily white boys
was Electra chose
      from the seven stars in the sky

Introduction

did Ilia bear fruit to the Strider
        was she found the handmaid of the Lar. . . .

did they project the rectilineal plane upwards
to the floor of heaven
had all
      within that reaching prism
           one patria:
      rooted clod or drifted star
      dog or dryad or
      man born of woman

did the sacred equation square the mundane site
was truth with fact conjoined
           did the earth-mother
blossom the stone lintels
           did *urvus* become *urbs*
did the bright share
           turn the dun clod
to the star plan
           did they parcel out
per scamna et strigas
           the *civitas* of God
that we should sprawl
           from Septimontium
a megalopolis that wills death?

Prophecies and myths, a supernatural birth, surveying and building, a history and a way of life issue in a question—rhetorical for Jones and the reader, real for the perplexed legionary who asks it, who guards a Jerusalem wall at the time of the Passion. The megalopolis wills the death of the *other*, the death of a troublesome Jew full of disruptive parabolic talk. But it also wills the death of Empire as the speaker has understood it and lived it: 'They used to say we marched for Dea Roma behind the wolf sign to eat up the world . . . but now they say

Introduction

the Quirinal Mars turns out to be no god of war but of armed peace.' The world of Jones' Roman poems is familiar enough: from the Pax Romana to the Pax Americana the distance in some ways is not very great. We are clearly in an area of backgrounds shared by any Westerner, Christian or otherwise. A mile away from where I write runs the Roman road to Colchester, down which Boudicca travelled to sack the Empire's British capital. On the same road, in the opposite direction, travelled the Christian religion out of Roman Jerusalem. Over my head fly the American jets from Bentwaters Air Base.

> Does the pontifex, do our lifted trumpets, speak to the city and the world to call the tribes to Saturnalia to set misrule in the curule chair, to bind the rejected fillet on the King of the Bean?

The pontifex does, the lifted trumpets do. But if we say so, we say so—like the legionary himself—entangling ourselves in a network of history and signs which, though we only half remember (as he only half anticipates), involves us, while we lament with him bad government, in the Twelfth Night feast, the cutting of a very special cake, the election of a lord, the adorning of a sacrificial victim.

David Jones' work begins and ends with victims. Himself a victim of the hellish violence of the Western Front, he manages in *In Parenthesis* to write an epic of the First World War that has at the centre of its fire-swept mazes an extraordinary and otherworldly calm. Taken entire—and I cannot, of course, give the whole of it in this selection—*In Parenthesis* produces an effect more characteristic, for example, of Benjamin Britten's settings of Wilfred Owen's poems in his *War Requiem* than of Owen's poems themselves. Its catharsis is shattering and lasting, but it does not induce the catharsis of tragedy. It is too Dantesque for that. Still less does it generate the kinetic emotions which some of its readers would like to find in it (which doesn't mean that we fail to count the dead: we do), nor yet does it dramatize the merely passive suffering that Yeats objected to in war poems. It

Introduction

redeems the time. 'I did not', says Jones in his Preface, 'intend this as a 'War Book'—it happens to be concerned with war. I should prefer it to be about a good kind of peace—but as Mandeville says, "Of Paradys ne can I not speken propurly I was not there; it is fer beyonde and that for thinketh me. And also I was not worthi." We find ourselves privates in foot regiments. We search how we may see formal goodness in a life singularly inimical, hateful, to us.' Jones bodies forth such a formal goodness in what he calls simply 'a shape in words'. 'I have only tried to make a shape in words, using as data the complex of sights, sounds, fears, hopes, apprehensions, smells, things exterior and interior, the landscape and paraphernalia of that singular time and of those particular men.'

It is in the middle books of *In Parenthesis* that Jones describes what he calls in his Preface 'the intimate, continuing, domestic life of small contingents of men, within whose structure Roland could find, and, for a reasonable while, enjoy, his Oliver'. The present volume, following the short poem which is printed out of chronological order for reasons which I think will be obvious, begins with Part 3 of *In Parenthesis*. In some notes made for an Argo recording of his poems, Jones says this about the section:

> Part 3 as a whole is concerned with the movement of a unit from billets to positions in the Front Line at Christmas-time 1915. What is narrated would apply to any infantry unit involved in the routine life of static trench-warfare, with the important qualification that the outward events and the inward feelings here evoked concern an *initial* experience. Immediately to the front of our forward trenches there was, just behind the German line, a copse called the Bois du Biez, and its straggling, leafless, December trees looming out of the mist or, by night, delineated for a moment by some starshell or gun flash or the moon, remain still in my vision.

The initial experience is an initiation in every way—for John Ball, for David Jones, and for the reader. The first two parts of *In Parenthesis* are stylistically fairly conventional and familiar to the

Introduction

reader of memoirs or novels about the war. There is also something tentative about them, almost, perhaps, groping, as a painter and engraver teaches himself the disciplines of his new art. With the explosion of a shell at the end of Part 2—and with a paragraph that anticipates the style of both Parts 3 and 7—we enter the section of *In Parenthesis* Jones calls, after Hopkins, 'Starlight order'. As with all of the other sections, the legend is from *The Gododdin* of Aneirin, the import of which is glossed by Jones in his notes. Gwyn Williams' characterization of Welsh verse, a text well-loved by critics of David Jones, is illuminating here (and even more so in relation to the form of *The Anathemata*). Poets like Aneirin, he tells us, 'were not trying to write poems that would read like Greek temples or even Gothic cathedrals but, rather, like stone circles or the contour-following rings of the forts from which they fought, with hidden ways slipping from one ring to another'. We certainly feel ourselves to be in such a situation in the third part of *In Parenthesis*, slipping from one trench to another, one road to another, stumbling at the edge of things, carried along by a prose modulating into verse modulating back into prose that Jones fashions to 'juxtapose, dovetail, web up, any number of concepts, and bovine lunar tricks'. It was very probably a difficult section for Jones to write, requiring, among other aids, the useful map reprinted here from hardback editions of *In Parenthesis* on which the author plotted the movement of troops through a remembered maze of trenches and roads and sodden fields. At the centre of that maze is a 'culture'—for David Jones, a loaded, technical, Spenglerian word. I have known few readers who were not deeply moved by the description of the troops' arrival, finally, 'at the termination of ways', and few who have not felt themselves to be assimilated, however briefly and vicariously, to the 'folk-life' and the 'people' here so beautifully evoked, to the 'culture already developed, already venerable and rooted'.

The fourth part of *In Parenthesis*, and this selection from it, includes the Boast of Dai Great-Coat, annotated by the author with a particularly meticulous care. Much that is implicit else-

Introduction

where is here made explicit in a remarkable set-piece which Jones associates with the boast of Taliessin at Maelgwn's court, with the boast of Widsith, with the boast of Arthur's porter, Glewlwyd, and with the boast in John viii. Because the annotation is here so detailed, this would seem to be a natural time to pause a moment over the notes and to recommend a method for making use of them. In his Preface to *In Parenthesis*, in which the notes are printed at the end of the book, Jones asks the reader 'to consult the notes with the text' as he regards 'some of them as integral to it'. In the Preface to *The Anathemata*, in which the notes are printed at the foot of the page, he says, 'I ask the reader, *when actually engaged upon the text*, to consult these glosses mainly or only on points of pronunciation. For other purposes they should be read separately.' It depends, I think, on the particular text. The second method will work satisfactorily for Part 3 of *In Parenthesis*, for example, but not so well for Dai's Boast or 'Rite and Fore-Time' from *The Anathemata*. The reader should decide for himself according to the often quite different demands of each section, each passage. For reasons of economy, the notes in this selection (which have been very slightly abridged) are printed at the end of each major section. If I were asked for *general* advice in making use of them, I believe it would be the opposite of W. H. Auden's in his review of *The Anathemata*: 'to read a section the first time very slowly, consulting every note, and then a second time without looking at one'. I would suggest that the reader get from the text whatever he can on an initial reading without consulting the notes. Where I am in agreement with Auden is over the obvious point that more than one reading of any Jones text is required. I would suggest consulting the notes in most cases on a second and subsequent readings. Perhaps it is only on a third or fourth reading that we begin to feel ourselves fairly confidently in possession of the information we need to get from the text all that is in it, and even then our 'possession of information' is likely to remain just that—nothing like the 'quality of knowing', as Kathleen Raine has called it, natural to the man who made the

Introduction

poems and wrote the notes. But I cannot imagine anyone interrupting a first reading of Part 7 of *In Parenthesis*, for example, to look up anything at all, even though Jones himself tells us to.

This seventh and concluding section of *In Parenthesis*, 'The five unmistakable marks', requires very little commentary. Though I have had to make several cuts in the text, each indicated by asterisks, I am certain the reader will feel in his bones the terrifying and relentless forward movement of the narrative in which the companions of John Ball are annihilated and he himself is wounded. The writing in this section is of a singular and overwhelming power. Jones has written in the notes for his recording that the phrase from Carroll's verse which forms the title of Part 7 had been in his head before and during the war and that 'wholly independent of context, it is pretty impossible for anyone of our tradition, on reading the words "the five unmistakable marks" for these five words not to evoke Five Wounds'. He continues as follows:

> Just as the fragments [read on the recording] from Part 3 are concerned with the *initial* experience of routine trench life so the fragments from Part 7 are concerned with the *initial* experience of participation in a large-scale offensive. Curiously enough, a woodland loomed to our immediate front in both cases, but there the resemblance ended. In Part 3 the little wood was just something seen behind the German lines—something remote and almost in another world. . . . Here, in Part 7, the woodland (Bois de Mametz) to our front was large and in full summer foliage and on undulating chalk downland, and now it was not a wood to be merely observed behind the German lines, but a strongly defended position that the Welsh Division (to which my unit belonged) was ordered to capture.

It is in these woods, at some point after 4.15 a.m. on 10 July 1916, that John Ball and the other straggling survivors of the first stages of the offensive action are ordered by Captain Marlow to dig in, in a passage (omitted here) directly following the death of Mr Jenkins when 'Sergeant T. Quilter', himself about to die,

Introduction

'takes over'. About the haunting appearance of the 'Queen of the Woods' near the end of this section, in a passage which is also the formal conclusion of In Parenthesis—elegiac and healing in contrast to the unforgettable description of carnage that has just preceded it—Jones has written:

> The tutelary spirit of the wood . . . bestows her gifts 'according to precedence'—that is, according to the hidden degrees of 'valour' of these men now dead, which obviously no living man could assess. For though there is a truth in what is meant by 'Death the Leveller' there is, I think, a far more important truth in seeing it the opposite way round. This I tried to express in the words: 'Life the leveller hugs her impudent equality—she may proceed at once to less discriminating zones.' One was acutely aware, in however unformulated a fashion, of something of this sort in the particular circumstances of actual combat.

Following the selections from In Parenthesis, I have chosen three from The Anathemata—four including the Preface to that work—and four from The Sleeping Lord. David Jones is always his own best introducer, and it is good to have sufficient room here to print the Preface to The Anathemata almost entire. I wish there were room for still more of the prose as there is a great deal of it that is important both in terms of what it illuminates in Jones' own work and what it tells us about the past and present of our civilization. I would urge the reader to get hold of Epoch and Artist and read at least the essays called 'Art and Sacrament', 'The Utile', and 'The Myth of Arthur', along with the incomparable letters to various periodicals over the years protesting or explaining one thing or another. But clearly enough, I think, in a volume of this kind, the poems themselves should be given all due precedence.

My first selection from The Anathemata is roughly the first half, minus the bracketed passage on hills, of 'Rite and Fore-Time', along with the conclusion of that section beginning 'Upon all fore-times'. We are once again, as in In Parenthesis, in the

Introduction

Arthurian 'King Pellam's Launde', though this time also in the London of the Second World War among men of that 'kind of diaspora', which Jones spoke of in the letter I quoted earlier to René Hague, that includes 'man-the-artist' and 'man-the-priest'. The 'cult-man', both Christian priest and his primitive prototype—and also, by analogy, the poet—lifts up 'an efficacious sign'. It is at this point we should pay careful attention to what Jones says in his preface about sign and sign-making, for on the 'efficaciousness' of signs—or on the lack of it—all else for him depends. At the beginning of *The Anathemata* we are among the 'rear-guard details', and 'late in time . . . at the sagging end and chapter's close' with the poet who is also a worshipper at a war-time Christmas mass and whose mind, 'in the time of the Mass', perhaps during 'those few seconds taken by the presbyter to move from the Epistle to the Gospel side', is 'set in motion by some action or word . . . to twist and double on its tracks, penetrate recesses and generally nose about'. His associations transport us rapidly from the rite, or Mass, by way of its institution in the Cenacle to the fore-time of pre-history and 'deliberations made out of time, before all oreogenesis'. It is important that the upper room and the table at which the Eucharist is instituted are described in terms of ship imagery, for this anticipates the long sea journeys and their ultimate meaning in 'Middle-Sea and Lear-Sea', which is included here entire, 'Angle-Land', 'The Lady of The Pool' and 'Keel, Ram, Stauros'. In his essay on Coleridge's 'Ancient Mariner', Jones appreciates 'the validity and rightness' of fourth-century patristic writers in 'perceiving that much in the Odysseus saga (and other Classical deposits) had correspondences to the voyaging of the Christian soul and in the argosy of the Son of God. . . . [They] saw amid-ships the image of the same salvific Wood. And not the yarded mast only, but the planking and timbers composing the vessel, so of the chief timber, the Keel.'

It is a cardinal belief of David Jones that in so far as man is man—and as he developed out of other forms, so may he develop into other forms—he is a maker, an artist, capable of

Introduction

the gratuitous and intransitive activities which are traced in the rest of this selection to some of their earliest manifestations: the Lascaux cave paintings, for example, and the Venus of Willendorf, which anticipates the statue of Athena in 'Middle-Sea and Lear-Sea' and prefigures the Queen of Heaven herself whose beauty outshines even that of Guenever at the midnight mass in 'Mabinog's Liturgy'. But Jones goes back in time beyond the Aurignacian culture of the Venus and the cave paintings to the merest ritual markings on covering stones of between 40,000 and 60,000 BC, telling us in his notes that where 'an element of the extra-utile and the gratuitous' exists then 'the artefacturer or artifex should be regarded as participating *directly* in the benefits of the Passion, because the extra-utile is *the* mark of man'. The '*dona eis requiem*' incanted toward the conclusion of this selection is 'For all WHOSE WORKS FOLLOW THEM'—the works 'that follow supernatural faith whereby the doers gain supernatural benefit', but also, by analogy, 'those *opera* which we call artefacts, which man alone can cause to be'. And as for 'man-the-technocrat' whose civilization follows the culture of 'man-the-artist' and 'man-the-priest', the signs are there for him to read if he is able. In the allegorical conclusion of his long letter in *Epoch and Artist* called 'Past and Present', Jones imagines a burying party and a salvage squad attempting to decipher 'what were still valid as signs, for some of us, when our front was finally rolled up'. He says of them: 'No matter how metamorphosed by a technocracy the full ramifications of which we cannot as yet guess, in so far as they are still men they will not altogether escape the things of man.'

But 'Rite and Fore-Time' has to do not only with the emergence of 'man-the-maker', but also with the emergence of the Island of Britain. *The Anathemata* asks, as it were, 'how does it happen that I come to be doing this thing—here, now?' The 'here' of it is crucial, and David Jones is a powerful poet of place. With the separation of Britain from the land mass of Europe and with the 'therapy and fertility' of her soils brought about by glaciation—Cronos breaking his ice, like the priest his wafer,

Introduction

according to the rubric *frangit per medium*—the creatures of the Fore-Time emerge into history as men of an island capable of agriculture and, as a result, capable of making a culture.

About 'Middle-Sea and Lear-Sea', the one section I am able to give here entire, Jones has written this in his notes for the Argo recording: 'Since about the sixth millennium BC Britain has been an Island, but it was not until very much later that the Narrows of the Channel were navigable. Hence it was by more westerly routes that certain ingredient parts of what "made us" came to our shores.' Dating events throughout with great exactitude, Jones takes us in this section from the death of Hector at Troy through an evocation of crucial periods in the history of Greece and Rome, including the mythical founding of Rome, to a meditation on the sculpted forms of women in sixth-century BC Greece and twelfth-century AD France which connects backwards to the passage in 'Rite and Fore-Time' on the Venus of Willendorf and forwards to Phidias' sculpture of Athena which serves Aegean mariners as 'land-mark for sea-course'. There follow two sea voyages, the first that of an 'old Pelasgian' and his crew who get their bearings from the statue of Athena, a 'Virgo Potens', as 'the overcast clears on a Mars' Venus-Day/Selene waxed, the sun in the Ram'—at the hour, that is, of Christ's death. The second voyage Jones describes in his Argo notes:

> A vessel in difficult weather [is] making for the tin-trade port in the vicinity of Land's End and the Lizard. The master of her is envisaged as an old padrone from the Aegean with his ship's company all from the Mediterranean. She is approaching the Island 'up-Channel', but, owing to the weather, has passed Bolerion (Land's End) so that when 'Albion's brume begins to thin away' her look-out sights Deadman (or Dodman) Point and she has to reverse her course under very adverse conditions, to make Mount's Bay. The whole point of all this is merely to indicate how it was by thalassic journeyings that in 'pre-history' contacts were established between us and the various cradle-lands of our culture.

Introduction

By the time we reach Jones' beautiful and delicate description of Guenever at the midnight Christmas Mass from 'Mabinog's Liturgy'—a passage, incidentally, that remained one of the author's favourites—a culture has established itself.

At the date envisaged Britain had received the Christian cultus centuries back; precisely when, we do not know, but we do know that in the fourth century that cult became the official cult of the Empire and that by the fifth and sixth centuries, *romanitas* and *Christianitas* were virtually interchangeable terms. Whether we regard this as fortunate or unfortunate is not here my concern, but in so far as this is what happened as an historic fact, it was very much my concern in writing *The Anathemata*. For, from the time when this cultus of the Christian ecclesia became the accepted mythos of the empire, our entire complex of heritages, pre-Celtic, Celtic, Romano-Hellenistic, Nordic or what you will, became, to this or that degree, fused to eventually emerge as Christendom with the Mass as its central *signum*. That is why *The Anathemata* is cyclic in character and however wide the circles the action of the Mass is central to it and in so far as a circle can be said to have a 'beginning' or an 'end', it begins and ends with the Mass.

We are left, finally, with the selections from *The Sleeping Lord*. Four of the nine poems from this volume are on Roman themes, all of them set in Jerusalem well before the date of Guenever's appearance at the Christmas Mass, set, indeed, at the time of the Passion itself. The poems derive from Jones' visit to the Holy Land during the period of the British Mandate. Singly, the British soldiers Jones saw in Palestine reminded him of those he had known some twenty years earlier on the Western Front, the men and shades who march through *In Parenthesis* from Calais to King Pellam's Launde. But, as he says in a letter to Saunders Lewis, 'in their full parade rig . . . the riot-shields aligned to cover the left side and in each right fist the half-grip of a stout baton [they] evoked not the familiar things of less than two decades back, but

Introduction

rather of two millennia close on. . . .' Because of this association, Jones' legionaries often talk like cockneys. More importantly, because of the association, his sympathy is extended to these uncomprehending agents of Imperial power so far from their homes (in Greece, in Rome, in Gaul) and so caught up in the convolutions of history. And yet in spite of what Imperial unity, the heterogeneous composition of the Roman forces, or the key word 'sacramentum' in the enlistment oath might prefigure, the things of Caesar are the things of Caesar, a boot is always a boot. As Jones has it in 'Middle-Sea and Lear-Sea', paraphrasing Augustine: ''Tis a great robbery—is empire.'

The essential dialectic of *The Sleeping Lord* is worked out between the position of the Tribune in 'The Tribune's Visitation' and that of the supplicant in the wonderful prayer to the Earth Mother in 'The Tutelar of the Place', both of which are included here. The Tribune articulates a position which is antithetical to Jones' own: he is the fact-man, the prototype of 'man-the-technocrat', a figure who, like Brasso in 'The Dream of Private Clitus', would 'knock sideways and fragmentate . . . dreamed unities and blessed conjugations' even as he confesses his own nostalgia for such things to the men of his command. Saying that he too 'could weep/for these Saturnian spells/and for the remembered things', the 'known-site' and 'vintage hymn', he none the less goes on to assert that he and they are detailed 'to discipline the world-floor/to a common level/till everything presuming difference/and all the sweet remembered demarcations/wither/to the touch of us/and know the fact of empire'. In 'The Tutelar of the Place'—initially conceived, according to the letter to Saunders Lewis, as a monologue spoken by a 'Gaulish soldier on the wall of Hierosolyma telling his mate of the homeland in Celtica'—a gentle and quiet voice at the very edge of the Empire, in Wales, resists everything the Tribune represents. And it may be well to remember that though this poem is written by the least 'political' of poets, it is also written by one who has said that 'there is a sense in which "Barbara Allen" is many times more "propagandist" than "Rule

Introduction

Britannia" ' ", and that 'the more real the thing, the more it will confound their politics'. For the Wales of the supplicant is also the Wales of the poet, the Wales of the present and recent past. A land threatened by Roman bureaucrats has become a land rendered by modern industry and its masters, less every year a 'differentiated site' of 'holy diversities'.

It is quite impossible to give a brief account of all that is going on in the Welsh poems from *The Sleeping Lord*. 'The Tutelar of the Place' anticipates 'The Hunt', and 'The Hunt' is really the first part of the title poem, only the ending of which can be included here. The chief figure in these last two poems, the dominant and disquieting presence, is that of Arthur. Deriving chiefly from the 'Culhwch and Olwen' tale in *The Mabinogion*, the Arthur of these poems becomes a complex and composite figure in whom the 'holy diversities' find their unity in 'blessed conjugations' and their embodiment in the hunter of the boar Trwyth and the Lord whose sleeping body is his land. Hero, King, and Lord, attended by his candle-bearer, his poet, and his priest, he is everything our megalopolitan technological society denies. Most of all he is *other*. He is The Sleeping Lord. About his source in *The Mabinogion* Jones has said: 'Though the theme itself is a common mythological theme stretching back to remote prehistory, here in this Welsh tale, its setting is a knowable, factual, precisely defined tract of country. In short, for all its marvels and numinous powers, its many strata and mystery, its narration "proceeds from the known to the unknown".' So does that of David Jones in 'The Hunt' and 'The Sleeping Lord'. The voice that issues from these poems, and particularly from the title poem, is, for one reader anyway—indeed for most readers who have declared themselves—absolutely compelling. It is a voice that speaks simultaneously from the very depths of the abyss of time and from our own moment as well, from our precarious ledge—linguistic, cultural and social—on the edge of that abyss. It is the voice of a visionary in an age when we need vision desperately but habitually settle, in our poetry as in our philosophy and our politics, for hopelessly meagre and

Introduction

impoverished substitutes. *Poiesis*, making, is for Jones a high calling—it is *the* human calling, it is definitive. As a Christian he can write: 'Unless man is of his essential nature a *poeta*, one who makes things that are signs of something, then the central act of the Christian religion is totally without meaning.' This in spite of his deeply tragic sense of a profound diminution in our ability to respond to sign, symbol, allusion, analogy, and what he regarded as the sacramental nature of all artists' juxtaposed forms in a time when, as he says in 'Rite and Fore-Time', 'the utile infiltration . . . is coming through each door'.

I hope this volume will extend considerably David Jones' readership and that new readers will be encouraged to begin for themselves a journey 'from the known to the unknown' as doubtless new readers of James Joyce were encouraged to do by T. S. Eliot's war-time selection from Joyce's work, *Introducing James Joyce*, on which the present selection is modelled. It was originally conceived immediately after Jones' death as an exclusively American book when his work was rapidly going out of print in the USA. When that crisis passed, when the Faber and Faber editions began to be distributed in the United States as well as Britain and Canada, it seemed that an introductory volume could still serve a useful purpose in all countries where Jones' work might find new readers. I think myself that his future audience will come from both sides of the Atlantic—in spite of the absence on either side of conditions conducive to poetry of a high stature—and that with any luck it will be a considerably wider audience than Jones himself would have guessed. He expresses surprise in a letter to Saunders Lewis that *The Anathemata* 'is better known and liked in the USA than *yn yr ynys hon* [in this our island]'. Reading this, one thinks immediately also of the increasingly visible and articulate readership in Canada. The diaspora Jones defined is probably larger than he knew. As for the gods, evidently they have returned to Wales. Sleeping there, they may wake. And our reasonable sentries at the gate of the city (at the mouth of the skull) had better spread the news.

A, a, a, DOMINE DEUS

I said, Ah! what shall I write?
I enquired up and down.
                       (He's tricked me before
with his manifold lurking-places.)
I looked for His symbol at the door.
I have looked for a long while
                       at the textures and contours.
I have run a hand over the trivial intersections.
I have journeyed among the dead forms
causation projects from pillar to pylon.
I have tired the eyes of the mind
                       regarding the colours and lights.
I have felt for His Wounds
                       in nozzles and containers.
I have wondered for the automatic devices.
I have tested the inane patterns
                       without prejudice.
I have been on my guard
                       not to condemn the unfamiliar.
For it is easy to miss Him
                       at the turn of a civilisation.

    I have watched the wheels go round in case I might see the living creatures like the appearance of lamps, in case I might see the Living God projected from the Machine. I have said to the perfected steel, be my sister and for the glassy towers I thought I felt some beginnings of His creature, but *A, a, a, Domine Deus*, my hands found the glazed work unrefined and the terrible crystal a stage-paste . . . *Eia, Domine Deus*.

                                            c. 1938 and 1966

FROM

In Parenthesis

seinnyessit e gledyf ym
penn mameu

Part 3

STARLIGHT ORDER

Men went to Catraeth, familiar with laughter.
The old, the young, the strong, the weak.

Proceed . . . without lights . . . prostrate before it . . . he begins without title, silently, immediately . . . in a low voice, omitting all that is usually said. No blessing is asked, neither is the kiss of peace given . . . he sings alone.²

Cloud shielded her bright disc-rising yet her veiled influence illumined the texture of that place, her glistening on the saturated fields; bat-night-gloom intersilvered where she shone on the mist drift,
when they paraded
   at the ending of the day, unrested
      bodies, wearied from the morning,
   troubled in their minds,
      frail bodies loaded over much,
'prentices bearing this night the full panoply, the complex paraphernalia of their trade.
The ritual of their parading was fashioned to austerity, and bore a new directness.
They dressed to an hasty alignment,
they did not come to the slope;
by a habit of their bodies, conforming to monosyllabic, low-voiced, ordering.
   They moved rather as grave workmen than as soldiers from their billets' brief shelter.

[35]

From In Parenthesis

For John Ball there was in this night's parading, for all the fear in it, a kind of blessedness, here was borne away with yesterday's remoteness, an accumulated tedium, all they'd piled on since enlistment day: a whole unlovely order this night would transubstantiate, lend some grace to. Knobbed nickel at under arm thumb at seam smart cut away from the small[3] (and hair on upper lip invests him with little charm) re-numbering re-dressing two-inch overlap pernickety poshers-up, drum-majors knashing in their Blancoed paradises, twisted pipe-clayed knots for square-pushing shoulders,[4] tin soldiers, toy soldiers, militarymen in rows—you somehow suffer the pain of loss—it's an ungracious way of life—buttocked lance-jacks crawling for the second chevron—Band-boys in The Wet[5]—the unnamable nostalgia of depots.

He would hasten to his coal-black love: he would breathe more free for her grimly embrace, and the reality of her. He was glad when they said to him—and the free form of it:

When you're ready No. 7—sling those rifles—move them on sergeant, remain two-deep on the road—we join 5, 6 and 8 at the corner—don't close up—keep your distance from No. 6—be careful not to close up—take heed those leading files—not to close on No. 6—you're quite ready?—very good.

Move on . . . move 'em on.

Get on . . . we're not too early.

Informal directness buttressed the static forms—ritual words made newly real.

The immediate, the nowness, the pressure of sudden, modifying circumstance—and retribution following swift on disregard; some certain, malignant opposing, brought intelligibility and effectiveness to the used formulae of command; the liturgy of their going-up assumed a primitive creativeness, an apostolic actuality, a correspondence with the object, a flexibility.

Back past the white board at the juncture of the ditches, the gossamer swaying camouflage to drape the night-lit sky. The bombardier was whistling at his work on No. 3. Night-lines[6]

Part 3: Starlight order

twinkle above the glistening vegetable damp: men standing illusive in the dark light about some systemed task, transilient, regularly spaced, at kept intervals, their feet firm stanced apart, their upper bodies to and fro . . . slid through live, kindly, fingers

cylindrical shining
death canistering
the dark convenient dump, momentarily piling.
 Horses draw out to the road, lightly, unballast—tail-board pins play free and road-sets flint for the striking, at slither and recover.
 One leaping up behind who cries out—tosses some bulging sack:
For the wagon lines[7]—forgot last night—
good night Dai.
Good night Mick.
Good night Master
may Barbara [St. B - patroness of gunners]
bless the bed that you go to
and keep
her partial suffrages against his evening hate.[8]
Good night Parrott
good night Bess.
Good night good night—buck up—he gets nasty later on.
Good night, bon swores 'Waladr. Nos dawch, Jac-y-dandi.[9]
Night night. [goodnight to you]

They halted for the hurrying team; envying the drivers their waiting beds.

No. 6 moved, just visible, in front.
 Guides met them at an appointed place; pilots who knew the charting of this gaining wilderness; the road continued its undeviating eastward thrust, its texture more tedious to the feet with each going forward; the road-pittings, irregularly filled, becoming now the greater surface. They passed a place

From In Parenthesis

where was a ruin, they heard muted voices: the dark seemed gaining on the hidden moon—No. 6, in front, no longer seen.

A fanned-flashing to the higher dislocations—how piteous the torn small twigs in the charged exposure: an instant, more intenser, dark.

Throbbing on taut ear-drum
boomed hollow out-rushing and the
shockt recoil
the unleashing
a releasing.

Far thuddings faintly heard in the stranger-world: where the road leads, where no man goes, where the straight road leads; where the road had led old men asleep on wagons beneath the green, girls with baskets, linen-palled, children dawdling from the Mysteries on a Sunday morning.

Field-battery flashing showed the nature of the place the kindlier night had hid: the tufted avenue denuded, lopt, deprived of height; stripped stumps for flowering limbs—this discontent makes winter's rasure creaturely and kind.

A sand-bagged barrier checks the road by half.

They were told to halt.

Rain began to fall.

A shielded lantern hung by the barrier, cast refracted ray like gusty rush-light gleam for under facets, on his Webley's lanyard-ring; on the rimless pince-nez of the other.

He was talking to the commander of No. 6; a huddled sentry, next them, by the wall of bags. The rain increased where they miserably waited, there was no sound at all but of its tiresome spatter; the clouded moon quite lost her influence, the sodden night, coal-faced. They lighted saturated cigarettes.

Wind gusts rose to swirl and frisk half-severed, swung branches; jammed wood split to twisted screechings. Away somewhere, gun with lifted muzzle, Jaguar-coughs, across the rain. While they wait in the weather by the barrier, and half doze over their rifle-stocks.

Part 3: Starlight order

Someone seemed to be stirring in front; they bunch their heads in the next file: Pass the message back—who—where's the sergeant—to move on.
 Stand fast you.
 Stand fast 2, 3 and 4.
 Move on No. 1—get 'em into file corporal—move on by section—put those cigarettes out—no lights past the barrier. Past the little gate.
 Mr. Jenkins watched them file through, himself following, like western-hill shepherd.
 Past the little gate,
into the field of upturned defences,
into the burial-yard—
the grinning and the gnashing and the sore dreading—nor saw he any light in that place.[10]
 Wind's high-rising, rustling inter-lined Burberry, damp-flapping across knee-joint.
 Jaguar-gun, wind carried, barks again from X zone.

In virid-bright illumining he sees his precious charge, singly going, each following each, fleecy coated, and they themselves playing the actor to their jackets on sheepwalk's lateral restricting, between the lopped colonnade.
 Shuts down again the close dark; the stumbling dark of the blind, that Breughel knew about—ditch circumscribed; this all depriving darkness split now by crazy flashing; marking hugely clear the spilled bowels of trees, splinter-spike, leper-ashen, sprawling the receding, unknowable, wall of night—the slithery causeway—his little flock, his armed bishopric, going with weary limbs.
 '44 Adams was the rear man in that filed-flock; who stopped suddenly, ill controlled and stumblingly, whose hinder-gear collided, in the fickle flashing with the near-stepping, of many thoughts care-full, head down bent platoon commander.
 Sorry sir they've—Get on man get on, you'll lose connection.

From In Parenthesis

Sorry sir they've stopped in front.

Pass up message from officer in rear—Message from in front sir—they've halted sir—to right of road sir—road blocked, sir.

So they stood waiting; thick-textured night cloaked.

So he dreamed where he slept where he leaned, on piled material in the road's right ditch.

Stepping over things in the way, can't lift knee high enough—it makes the thigh ache so—more of them in front as far as you can see—can't go to left or right—this restricting corridor—higher ones, hurdles on 'jerks-ground':

Up, up—o-ver

Up pup—o-verr.

Gorilla-sergeant, in striped singlet, spring-toed, claps his hands like black-man-master: Get over—you Ball—you cowson.

Obstacles on jerks-course made of wooden planking—his night phantasm mazes a pre-war, more idiosyncratic skein, weaves with stored-up very other tangled threads; a wooden donkey for a wooden hurdle is easy for a deep-sleep trans-formation-fay to wand

carry you on dream stuff

up the hill and down again

show you sights your mother knew,

show you Jesus Christ lapped in hay with Uncle Eb and his diamond dress-stud next the ox and Sergeant Milford taking his number, juxtapose, dovetail, web up, any number of concepts, and bovine lunar tricks.

Hurdles on jerks-course all hard-edged for inefficient will not obtain the prize ones, who beat the air; wooden donkeys for the shins of nervous newcomer to the crowded night-class, step over to get your place beside Mirita; it's a winding mile between hostile matter from the swing-door, in and out the easel forest in and out barging, all of 'em annoyed with the past-pushing with clumsy furniture. Stepping over Miss Weston's thrown about belongings. Across his night dream the nightmare awaking:

Move on—get a move on—step over—up over.

And sleepy eyed see Jimmy Grove's[11] irregular bundle-

Part 3: Starlight order

figure, totter upward labouringly, immediately next in front, his dark silhouette sways a moment above you—he drops away into the night and your feet follow where he seemed to be. Each in turn labours over whatever it is—this piled brokenness—dragged over and a scared hurrying on—the slobber was ankle-deep where you found the road again.

Mr. Jenkins read his watch while he waited for the last man; they'd been going just an hour; he followed on again after old Adams of Section 4. Intermittent gun flashing had ceased; nothing at all was visible; it still rained in a settled fashion, acutely aslant, drenching the body; they passed other bodies, flapping, clinking, sodden; moving west, moving invisible, never known, no word said, no salutation. A straggler following—fleet-passing sound-wraith, coughing hollowly in his running to catch up; coughing like strangers do at night in some other room, in a stranger-house; and some other follows him, hurrying faster by—still coughing far down the road, heard in wind lull—ought to do something about it; see the M.O. or something, it's ridiculous not to do something about it . . . out on a night like this. A cold place—O, there couldn't be a colder place for my love to wander in—and it's only early on, you wait till March and the lengthening light on the low low lands.[12]

Mind the hole sir—mind the hole, keep left—go slower in front—they've halted sir.

He pushed forward to investigate.

Is that you sir, Sergeant Snell sir, we've lost connection with No. 6, sir—they must have turned off sir—back there sir.

Where's the guide.

With No. 6 sir.

Lovely for them—we'd better keep the road, get to the rear, see no one falls out, see them all up—move on No. 7, don't lose connection—wait for the man behind—move on.

There's no kind light to lead: you go like a motherless child—goddam guide's done the dirty, and is our Piers Dorian Isambard

[41]

From In Parenthesis

Jenkins—adequately informed—and how should his inexperience not be a broken reed for us—and fetch up in Jerry's bosom.
    Slower in front—slower,
not so regardless of this perturbation in the rear; for each false footfall piles up its handicap proportionately backward, and No. 1's mole hill is mountainous for No. 4; and do we trapse dementedly round phantom mulberry bush . . . can the young bastard know his bearings.

Keep well to left—take care with these messages.
    About their feet the invisible road surface split away in a great, exactly drawn circle; they felt its vacuous pitness in their legs, and held more closely to the banked-up solid.

The rain stopped.
She drives swift and immaculate out over, free of these obscuring waters; frets their fringes splendid.
A silver hurrying to silver this waste
silver for bolt-shoulders
silver for butt-heel-irons
silver beams search the interstices, play for breech-blocks underneath the counterfeiting bower-sway; make-believe a silver scar with drenched tree-wound; silver-trace a festooned slack; faery-bright a filigree with gooseberries and picket-irons[13]— grace this mauled earth—
transfigure our infirmity—
shine on us.
I want you to play with
and the stars as well.[14]
    Received,
curtained where her cloud captors
pursue her bright
pursue her darkly
detain her—
when men mourn for her, who go stumbling, these details for the ambuscade praise her, for an adjutrix; like caved robbers on

[42]

Part 3: Starlight order

a Mawddwy hill—the land waste as far as English Maelor; green girls in broken keeps have only mastiff-guards—like the mademoiselle at Croix Barbée.[15]

Transferred Warwick subaltern with his Welsh platoon passed them in the moon, his thoughts on green places where the counties meet; they're still secure at Bourton-on-the-Water. She did her knitting to this comforter staying with Aunt Mildred in Stretton—they left Tite Street to avoid the raids.
The precious: she's made it of double warp.
The cowsons: they've banned 'em[16]—they do deaden the sound a bit—but not much use hearing It coming.
  The Mercian dreamer and his silent men all pass in turn, followed on by more, who, less introspect, wish a brief good night.
  It's cushy[17] mate, it's cushy—
it's cushy up there but
buck up past Curzon Post—he has it taped.
  Good night chum.
  Good night.

The repeated passing back of aidful messages assumes a cadency.
Mind the hole
mind the hole
mind the hole to left
hole right
step over
keep left, left.
  One grovelling, precipitated, with his gear tangled, struggles to feet again:
Left be buggered.
  Sorry mate—you all right china?—lift us yer rifle—an' don't take on so Honey—but rather, mind
the wire here[18]
mind the wire
mind the wire
mind the wire.

[43]

From In Parenthesis

Extricate with some care that taut strand—it may well be you'll sweat on its unbrokenness.

Modulated interlude, violently discorded—mighty, fanned-up glare, to breach it: light orange flame-tongues in the long jagged water-mirrors where their feet go, the feet that come shod, relief bringing—bringing release to these from Wigmore and Woofferton. Weary feet: feet bright, and gospelled, for these, of Elfael and Ceri.

We're relieving the Borderers—two platoons of their 12th thet was—in wiv the Coldstreams[19]—relieved be our 14th.

Sergeant Snell was informed as to the disposition of units.

The colonnade to left and right kept only shorn-off column shafts, whose branchy capitals strew the broken sets. Where roofless walls, reinforced with earth-filled sacks fronted the road, on a board, moon lighted, they read as they filed past:

TO
MOGGS HOLE
NO LOITERING BY DAY

and from its peg, a shell-case swung,[20] free of the sand-bagged wall.

Sometimes his bobbing shape showed clearly; stiff marionette jerking on the uneven path; at rare intervals he saw the whole platoon, with Mr. Jenkins leading.

Wired dolls sideway inclining, up and down nodding, fantastic troll-steppers in and out the uncertain cool radiance, amazed crook-back miming, where sudden chemical flare, low-flashed between the crazy flats, flood-lit their sack-bodies, hung with rigid properties—
the drop falls,
you can only hear their stumbling off, across the dark proscenium.

So they would go a long while in solid dark, nor moon, nor battery, dispelled.

Part 3: Starlight order

Feet plodding in each other's unseen tread. They said no word but to direct their immediate next coming, so close behind to blunder, toe by heel tripping, file-mates; blind on-following, moving with a singular identity.

Half-minds, far away, divergent, own-thought thinking, tucked away unknown thoughts; feet following file friends, each his own thought-maze alone treading; intricate, twist about, own thoughts, all unknown thoughts, to the next so close following on.

He hitched his slipping rifle-sling for the hundredth time over a little where the stretched out surface skin raw rubbed away at his clavicle bone. He thought he might go another half mile perhaps—it must be midnight now of some day of the week. He turned his tired head where the sacking-shield swayed.

Where a white shining waned between its hanging rents, another rises and another; high, unhurrying higher, clear, pale, light-ribbons; very still-bright and bright-showered descent.

Spangled tapestry swayed between the uprights; camouflage-net, meshed with plunging star-draught.

Bobbing night-walkers go against the tossing night-flares.

Intermittent dancing lights betray each salient twist and turn; tiny flickers very low to the south—their meandering world-edge prickt out bright.

Rotary steel hail spit and lashed in sharp spasms along the vibrating line; great solemn guns leisurely manipulated their expensive discharges at rare intervals, bringing weight and full recession to the rising orchestration.

As suddenly the whole world would slip back into a mollifying, untormented dark; their aching bodies knew its calm.

What moved in front is rigid with a clumsy suddenness:
Message back—they've halted mate.
What's that.
We've got to halt, pass it back.
He just muttered halt without a turn of the head.

From **In Parenthesis**

Get on get on—we'll lose connection.
They've halted I tell you, pass it back.
Dark chain of whisperings link by link jerked each one motionless.
A mile you say?
About a mile sir—straight on sir—machine gun, sir, but they're spent, most of 'em—but further on sir, by Foresters Lane—he's got a fixed-rifle on the road[21]—two of our people—last night sir.
The Borderer sergeant bid good night and passed like his predecessors toward the west.
'Night sergeant.
'Night chaps—yes cushy—but buck up on the road.

The hide and seek of dark-lit light-dark yet accompanied their going; the journeying moon yet curtained where she went.
Once when her capricious shining, when she briefly aided them, John Ball raised up his head:
In the cleft of the rock they served Her in anticipation—and over the hill-country that per-bright Shiner stood for Her rod-budding (he kept his eyes toward the swift modulations of the sky, heaven itinerant hurrying with his thought hasting)—but that was a bugger of a time ago.[22]

Nuvver 'ole mate—pass it back—largish an' all—look where yer going.
He took notice of his stepping, his eyes left their star-gazing.
Slime-glisten on the churnings up, fractured earth pilings, heaped on, heaped up waste; overturned far throwings; tottering perpendiculars lean and sway; more leper-trees pitted, rown-sepykèd out of nature, cut off in their sap-rising.
Saturate, littered, rusted coilings, metallic rustlings, thin ribbon-metal chafing—rasp low for some tension freed; by rat, or wind, disturbed. Smooth-rippled discs gleamed, where gaping craters, their brimming waters, made mirror for the sky procession—bear up before the moon incongruous souvenirs.

[46]

Part 3: Starlight order

Margarine tins sail derelict, where little eddies quivered, wind caught, their sharp-jagged twisted lids wrenched back.

From chance hardnesses scintilla'd strikings, queer reboundings at spiteful tangent sing between your head and his.

That one went up at an unexpected nearness. The faraway dancing barrier surprisingly much nearer; you even hear the dull report quickly upon the uprising light; and now, right where they walked, at sudden riot against your unsuspecting ear-drums, a Vicker's team discovers its position, by low builded walls of sacks; and men worked with muffled hammerings of wood on wood; and the front files pause again.

Yes—who are you—get your men into cover while they're halted. He flashed his torch on the other's uniform; which near brightness made them hug in closer, their apprentice-wisdom shocked.

A bleeding brass hat.

The bastard'll have us all blown up—softly, and consider his plenary powers, it's that cissy from Brigade, the one wat powders.

You've lost your guide—you can read the map, anyway, it's a plumb straight road—you've three hundred yards to the communication trench—turn left into Sandbag Alley—right at the O.B.L.[23]—left into Oxford Street—get along quickly—he has us enfiladed.

Thank you sir, good night sir.

He lights another cigarette. His match is like a beacon in this careful dark. His runner emerges from the bags on the left.

Yes sir—to the car sir?

No, leave me at Lansdowne Post—tell him to bring it up Foresters—Oh yes he can, perfectly well—tell him mess is at 8.0 not 8.30.

And the servants of the rich are off on the word: Bo!—what I mean to say is you don't want to lose the job
nor 'get returned'

From **In Parenthesis**

to march with these
gay companions—
He's near enough already—he passes most horribly close—
and these go out to jig with him on slanting floors.

No. 7 to move on—not far now little children—try to keep the pace.
 The road, broken though it was, seemed a firm causeway cutting determinedly the insecurity that lapped its path, sometimes the flanking chaos overflowed its madeness, and they floundered in unstable deeps; chill oozing slime high over ankle; then they would find it hard and firm under their feet again, the mason work in good order, by some freak, intact. Three men, sack-buskined to the hips, rose like judgment wraiths out of the ground, where brickwork still stood and strewn red dust of recent scattering dry-powdered the fluid earth; and your nostrils draw on strangely pungent air.

No sir—further on sir, but you'd better go by the trench, he's on this bit—yes to Pioneer Keep, then into the front line—it's right of this road—the O.B.L. sir?—we stopt using it a week back sir, he knocked it flat when they went over from The Neb—you can chance the road sir, but he's on it—all the time—three of the Coldstreams, only yesterday—he's traversing now—better get in, sir.
 He filed the leading section behind low harbouring earth; 2, 3 and 4 following; and last came Sergeant Snell, his mess-tin like a cullender.
 And he quietened down—nothing but a Lewis gun, far away.

I think we'll use the road—move out No. 4—move out the next section—move on—get those men out, sergeant—move on—No. 4 leading.
 They stepped delicately from this refuge.
 They've halted in front sir.

Part 3: Starlight order

German gunner, to and fro, leisurely traversed on his night-target.

Sergeant Snell with No. 4 crumpled, low crouched, in ineffectual ditch-shelter.

All right in front—you all right Sergeant Snell?—move your men on, sergeant.

Pass up the message—move on in front—move on immediately.

Pass it up—what's the game.

There's a windy tripehound.

Step on it for christ's sake, you're holding up Duration.

And this burst spent, they moved on again, alertness bringing new strength to their ill condition; awareness for their aching limbs: their great frailty was sufficient body for the forming of efficient act.

With his first traversing each newly scrutinised his neighbour; this voice of his Jubjub gains each David his Jonathan; his ordeal runs like acid to explore your fine feelings; his near presence at break against, at beat on, their convenient hierarchy.

Lance-Corporal Lewis sings where he walks, yet in a low voice, because of the Disciplines of the Wars.[24] He sings of the hills about Jerusalem, and of David of the White stone.[25]

Now when a solitary star-shell rose, a day-brightness illumined them; long shadows of their bodies walking, darkening out across the fields; slowly contracting with the light's rising, grotesquely elongating with its falling—this large lengthening is one with all this other.

Machine-gunner in Gretchen Trench[26] remembered his night target. Occasionally a rifle bullet raw snapt like tenuous hide whip by spiteful ostler handled. On both sides the artillery was altogether dumb.

Appear more Lazarus figures, where water gleamed between dilapidated breastworks, blue slime coated, ladling with wooden ladles; rising, bending, at their trench dredging. They speak low.

From **In Parenthesis**

Cold gurgling followed their labours. They lift things, and a bundle-thing out; its shapelessness sags. From this muck-raking are singular stenches, long decay leavened; compounding this clay, with that more precious, patient of baptism; chemical-corrupted once-bodies. They've served him barbarously—poor Johnny—you wouldn't desire him, you wouldn't know him for any other. Not you who knew him by fire-light nor any of you cold-earth watchers, nor searchers under the flares.[27]

Each night freshly degraded like traitor-corpse, where his heavies flog and violate; each day unfathoms yesterday unkindness; dung-making Holy Ghost temples.

They bright-whiten all this sepulchre with powdered chloride of lime. It's a perfectly sanitary war.

R.E.s, sir—yes sir, Sandbag Alley—leads into the O.B.L. sir—water-logged all the way sir—well above the knee sir—best keep the road—turn off left at Edgware, right at Hun Street sir—straight to the front line sir, brings you out be 'P' Sap, you couldn't miss it sir, not if you wanted to—we've a bit of a dump at the turn sir—our sergeant's there, with a carrying party—only just gone up sir.

The sapper returned to his baling; they heard him and his mates low mumbling; they heard the freed passage of the water sluice away, with the dreadful lifting-out of obstacles.

Close up in file and halt, pass it back quietly—move on until the last man is in the trench, and stand fast—pass it up when you're all in—see to that, sergeant.

Mr. Jenkins found his speech low-toned and regulated, lest he should wake the slumbering secrets of that place. A pallid Very-light climbed up from away in front. This gate of Mars armipotente, the grisly place, like flat painted scene in top-lights' crude disclosing. Low sharp-stubbed tree-skeletons, stretched slow moving shadows; faintest mumbling heard just at ground level. With the across movement of that light's

[50]

Part 3: Starlight order

shining, showed long and strait the dark entry, where his ministrants go, by tunnelled ways, whispering.[28]

Step down—
step down and keep a bit left—keep your rifles down—mind the wire
mind the wire—
be careful of the wire.

The long professed sergeant of engineers; '04, Time Expired, out since the Marne; tempered to night watchings, whole armoured against this sorry place; considerate of sluices, revetting frames and corrugated iron; of sapping to his second line, of mines and countermines, who dreamed of pontoons in open places, of taking over from the cavalry; stood at the trench head, and kindly, in a quiet voice, guided their catechumen feet:

Seem pretty bitched—but they'll soon shape—get 'em in quickly corporal, it's not too healthy here.

Far gone before the mind could register the passage, shells of high velocity over their trench-entering: Four separate, emptying detonations.

He's on Mogg's again—he's using H.E.—hope to christ the relief's through—it's that blasted Euston Road tramway that attracts him.

Edgware Trench, like a river's lock-gates, marked a new mood for the highway, which bore on still straightly; but from this bar, to litter its receding eastward surface, were strewn, uncleared, untouched, the souvenirs of many days; by no one walked upon, except perhaps some more intrepid Runner or charmed-life Linesman, searching, prying, cat-eyed, high and low diligently nosing, like pearl of great price seeker, for his precious rubber coiling—or more rarely a young gentleman from Division made bold by other considerations. He raises hell if one is late for mess.

All in sir—last man up—pass it up to move on—to move along—to move on quietly.

From In Parenthesis

You step down between inward inclining, heavily bulged, walls of earth; you feel the lateral slats firm foothold. Squeaking, bead-eyed hastening, many footed hurrying, accompanying each going forward.

Break in the boards—pass it back.

The fluid mud is icily discomforting that circles your thighs; and Corporal Quilter sprawls full length; two of them help him to his feet, his rifle like a river-bed salvaged antique—which dark fumbling assistance brings the whole file to a standstill—who call out huskily, to move on; to get a move on, and now perversely—slower in front, go slower in front.

John Ball cries out to nothing but unresponsive narrowing earth. His feet take him upward over high pilings—down again to the deep sludge. There is no one before him where the way loses its identity in a network of watery ditches; he chooses the middle ditch, seen in the light's last flicker. Beneath his feet, below the water, he feels again the wooden flooring, and round the next bend in another light's rising the jogging pack of Aneirin Lewis—and heard him singing, very low, as he went.

So they will continue: each step conditioned, every yard subtly other in direction from the last, their bodies' angle and inclination strictly determined by this winding corridor, by the floor's erratic levels. At some points new built walls rose above their heads, their feet going confidently on neat laid engineer work—but here again hastily thrown-up earth insufficiently filled wide breaches, and they went exposed from the waist upward.

Pass it along—stand to left of trench—make way for carrying party.

Gretchen Trench gunner resumes his traversing. They low-crouched on haunches where the duckboard slats float. The freshly-set sand-bags fray and farrow; the hessian jets loose earth—clammy sprinklings, cold for your vertebrae. You hug lower crumpled against the quivering hurdle-stake.[29]

Evidently that carrying party had decided to halt. Gretchen-

Part 3: Starlight order

trench gunner lowered his sights to 'Y' target, making taller men stoop, hunchbackwise out in 'P' sap.

Peering up from their crouching, feel solid, shadowy, careful past-pushing, leg moving rigid, awkward, lengthway, negotiating.

The night was at its darkest, you couldn't see the nearest object.

Go easy chum—
keep low here—steady a bit, lift up a bit—all right your end?—you over—over—bit of a weight Joe.

They go like that, like bleedin' lead.

Metalled eyelet hole in waterproof pall hanging glides cold across your upward tilted cheek with that carrying party's unseen passing—the smell of iodine hangs about when it's used so freely.

You can hear the stumbling, dead-weighted, bearers, very tortuously make winding progress back; low-voiced questioned, here and there, by these waiting, latest ones.

Private Watcyn calls Lance-Corporal Lewis from round an earth wall's turn, who nudges Private Ball who drags forward saturated limbs; water pours from his left boot as he lifts it clear. Scrapings and dull joltings, heavy, ill-controlled lurching, disturbed water gurgles with each man's footfall; they move ten yards further.

Mind the wire, china[30]
        —keep yourself low.

Bodies move just at head level, outside the trench; hollow unreal voices, reaching the ear unexpectedly, from behind or round the traverse bend, like the shouting at the immediate door comes on you from a far window:

I've found it Bertie, I've got 'D' and 'C'.

Telephonic buzzing makes the wilderness seem curiously homely; the linesman's boot implicates someone's tackle passing.

Sorry son—sorry.

He continues his song; he beats time with his heels thudding the trench-wall, his trade in his lap:

[53]

From In Parenthesis

Kitty Kitty isn't it a pity
 in the City[31]—it's a bad break, Bertie.
They bend low over, intently whistling low, like a mechanic's mate. They secure it with rubber solution; they pick their way, negotiating unseen wire, they remember the lie of the land with accuracy; they kick tins gratuitously, they go with light hearts; they walk naked above the fosse, they despise a fenced place; they are warned for Company Office. They pull at his decanter while he sleeps; they elude quartermasters; they know the latest—whispered however so low.[32]

The night dilapidates over your head and scarlet lightning annihilates the nice adjustment of your vision, used now to, and cat-eyed for the shades. You stumble under this latest demonstration; white-hot nine-inch splinters hiss, water-tempered, or slice the cross-slats between his feet—you hurry in your panic, which hurrying gives you clumsy foothold, which falling angers you, and you are less afraid; you call them all bastards—you laugh aloud.

Shrapnel salvos lift to the front line; rapid burst on burst. After a while it would be quiet again. There was no retaliation—not this early on.

And where the earth-works forked, the clipt hierarchic word, across the muted half-sounds connatural to the place, in some fashion reformed them, brought to them some assurance and token of normality.

Pass Relief.

Major Cantelupe?—no sir—going his rounds sir—th' adjutant?—at mess, sir.

The drawn back sacking loosed a triangle of consoling candle light.

He comes again; they stir where they heap like sawn logs diversely let to lie; they assemble their bodies on the narrow footing; they move on without sensation. The water's level is higher with each turn of the trench; the detached boards, on being trod on, at the nearer end, rise perpendicular for your

[54]

Part 3: Starlight order

embarrassment. Another salvo for the line—Curzon Post—Mogg's Hole.

And now at another forked-way, voices, and heavy material in contact, as if a gardener made firm a sloping pleasance; and someone coughs restrainedly and someone sings freely:

> O dear what can the matter be
> O dear what can the matter be
> O dear what can the matter be
> Johnny's so long at the Fair.

And from these also, the file moves on; the sound of them, and his singing, like some unexpected benignity you come on at a street-bend.

Until dim flickerings light across; to fade where the revetment changes direction, and overhead wire catches oblique ray cast up, and you know the homing perfume of wood burned, at the termination of ways; and sense here near habitation, a folk-life here, a people, a culture already developed, already venerable and rooted.

Follow on quietly No. 7—file in quietly—not such a pandemonium to advertise our advent.

You turn sharp left; the space of darkness about you seems of different shape and character; earth walls elbow at you in a more complicated way. You stand fast against the parados.

And you too are assimilated, you too are of this people—there will be an indelible characterization—you'll tip-toe when they name the place.

Stand fast against the parados and let these eager bundles drag away hastily; and one turns on his going-out: Good night china—there's some dryish wood under fire-step[33]—in cubby-hole—good night.

Cushy—cushy enough—cushy, good night.

Good night kind comrade.

And the whole place empties; the narrow space clears. You

From In Parenthesis

feel about in the emptied darkness of it. They lose little time to make off, to leave you in possession.

Any of No. 7 here—Corporal Quilter here—Lance-Corporal Lewis—is Mathews here?
All of No. 1, sergeant—No. 1 Section complete, sergeant.
He posts his first night-sentries, there are ambiguous instructions; you will be relieved in two hours, the pass word is Prickly Pear.
And he, John Ball, his feet stayed-up above disintegrating earth —his breast at ground level. How colder each second you get stuck here after the sweat of it, and icy tricklings at every cavity and wherever your finger-tips stray, the slug surface. He buried each hand in his great-coat sleeves, habit-wise; the sagged headers sloped the parapet for a stall.
His eyeballs burned for the straining, was any proper object for the retina in all that blind night-drift, and sergeant said to keep a sharp look-out—to report any hostile movement—and the counter-sign is
Prickly Pear
Prickly Pear
not to forget
important not to forget; important to keep your eyes open.

The light they sent up from the third bay[34] down, sinks feebly snuffed out in the weather, a yard before our wire; but its pallid arc sufficiently defines the paved way, preserving its camber and its straight-going from us to him; enough to shine on, long enough to show heaped-on rust heap, dripping water, like rained-on iron briary.
Peg sprawled tentacles, with drunken stakes thrust up rigid from the pocked earth. And to his immediate front, below the shelving ramp, a circular calm water graced the deep of a Johnson hole;[35] corkscrew-picket-iron half submerged, as dark excalibur, by perverse incantation twisted. And there, where the wire was thinnest: bleached, swaying, the dyed

Part 3: Starlight order

garment—like flotsam shift tossed up, from somebody other's dereliction.

At intervals lights elegantly curved above his lines, but the sheet-rain made little of their radiance. He heard, his ears incredulous, the nostalgic puffing of a locomotive, far off, across forbidden fields; and once upon the wind, from over his left shoulder, the nearer clank of trucks, ration-laden by Mogg's Hole.

    And the rain slacks at the wind veer
                      and she half breaks her cloud cover.

    He puts up a sufficient light dead over the Neb; and in its moments hanging, star-still, shedding a singular filament of peace, for these fantastic undulations.

    He angled rigid; head and shoulders free; his body's inclination at the extreme thrust of the sap head; outward toward them, like the calm breasts of her, silent above the cutwater,
foremost toward them
and outmost of us, and
brother-keeper, and ward-watcher;
his mess-mates sleeping like long-barrow sleepers, their
dark arms at reach.
Spell-sleepers, thrown about anyhow under the night.
And this one's bright brow turned against your boot leather,
tranquil as a fer sídhe sleeper, under fairy tumuli, fair as Mac Og sleeping.[36]

Who cocks an open eye when you stamp your numbed feet on the fire-step slats,
who tells you to stow it,
to put a sock in it,
to let a man sleep o' nights
—and redistributes his cramped limbs, and draws closer-over his woollen comforter.

    You shift on the boards a little to beat your toes against the revetment where this other one sits upright, wakeful and less fastidious, at an angle of the bay; who speaks without turning his

From In Parenthesis

head to you, his eyes set on the hollow night beyond the parados, he nursing his rifle, the bayonet's flat to his cheek-bone; his syntax of the high hills—and the sharp inflexion:

Starving night indeed—important to maintain the circulation—there's starving for you—important to keep the circulation.

Yes corporal.
Can you see anything, sentry.
Nothing corporal.
'01 Ball is it, no.
Yes corporal.
Keep a sharp outlook sentry—it is the most elementary disciplines—sights at 350.
Yes corporal.
300 p'r'aps.
Yes corporal.

Starving as brass monkeys—as the Arctic bear's arse—Diawl![37]—starved as Pen Nant Govid, on the confines of hell. Unwise it is to disturb the sentinel.

Do dogs of Annwn glast[38] this starving air—do they ride the trajectory zone, between the tangled brake above the leaning walls.

This seventh gate is parked[39] tonight.
His lamps hang in this black cold and hang so still; with this still rain slow-moving vapours wreathe to refract their clear ray—like through glassy walls that slowly turn they rise and fracture—for this fog-smoke wraith they cast a dismal sheen.[40]

What does he brew in his cauldron,
over there.
What is it like.
Does he watch the dixie-rim.
Does he watch—
the Watcher.
Does he stir his Cup—he blesses no coward's stir over there.
Does he watch for the three score hundred sleeping, or bent to their night tasks under the wall. In the complex galleries his

[58]

Part 3: Starlight order

organisation in depth[41] holds many sleeping, well-watched-for sleepers under the night flares.[42]

Old Adams, Usk, sits stark, he already regrets his sixty-two years. His rifle-butt is a third foot for him,[43] all three supports are wood for him, so chill this floor strikes up, so this chill creeps to mock his bogus 'listing age.

Forty-five—christ—forty-five in Her Jubilee Year, before the mothers of these pups had dugs to nourish them.

He grips more tightly the cold band of his sling-swivel; he'd known more sodden, darker ways, below the Old Working. He shifts his failing flanks along the clammy slats, he settles next his lance-jack, he joins that muted song; together they sing low of the little cauldron, together they commemorate *Joni bach*.[44]

You draw out warm finger-tips:
Your split knuckles fumbling, foul some keen, chill-edged, jack-spike jutting.
You could weep like a child,
you employ the efficacious word,[45]
to ease frustration;
be rid of,
last back-breaking straws.

At 350—slid up the exact steel, the graduated rigid leaf precisely angled to its bed.

You remember the word of the staff instructor whose Kinross teeth bared; his bonnet awry, his broad bellow to make you spring to it; to pass you out with the sixty-three parts properly differentiated.[46]

You very gradually increase the finger-pressure to-ward and up-ward.

The hollow-places and the upright things give back their mimicry, each waking other, shockt far out. Short before his parapet, disturbed wire tangs oddly for the erratic ricochet.

You draw back the bolt, you feel 'the empty' hollow-lob, light against your boot lacing, you hear the infinitesimal disturbance of water in the trench drain.

From In Parenthesis

    And the deepened stillness as a calm, cast over us—a potent influence over us and him—dead-calm for this Sargasso dank, and for the creeping things.
    You can hear the silence of it:
you can hear the rat of no-man's-land
rut-out intricacies,
weasel-out his patient workings,
scrut, scrut, sscrut,
harrow-out earthly, trowel his cunning paw;
redeem the time of our uncharity, to sap his own amphibious paradise.
    You can hear his carrying-parties rustle our corruptions through the night-weeds—contest the choicest morsels in his tiny conduits, bead-eyed feast on us; by a rule of his nature, at night-feast on the broken of us.
    Those broad-pinioned;
blue-burnished, or brinded-back;
whose proud eyes watched
              the broken emblems
droop and drag dust,
suffer with us this metamorphosis.
    These too have shed their fine feathers; these too have slimed their dark-bright coats; these too have condescended to dig in.
    The white-tailed eagle at the battle ebb,
                  where the sea wars against the river[47]
the speckled kite of Maldon
and the crow
have naturally selected to be un-winged;
to go on the belly, to
sap   sap   sap
with festered spines, arched under the moon; furrit with whiskered snouts the secret parts of us.
    When it's all quiet you can hear them:
scrut scrut scrut
when it's as quiet as this is.
    It's so very still.

Part 3: Starlight order

Your body fits the crevice of the bay in the most comfortable fashion imaginable.

It's cushy enough.

The relief elbows him on the fire-step: All quiet china?—bugger all to report?—kipping mate?—christ, mate—you'll 'ave 'em all over.

From Part 4

KING PELLAM'S LAUNDE

Like an home-reared animal in a quiet nook, before his day came . . . before entering into the prison of earth . . . around the contest, active and defensive, around the fort, around the steep-piled sods.

John Ball, relieved for sentry, stood to his breakfast. He felt cheese to be a mistake so early in the morning. The shared bully was to be left in its tin for the main meal; this they decided by common consent. The bread was ill-baked and sodden in transit. There remained the biscuits; there remained the fourth part of a tin of jam; his spoonful of rum had brought him some comfort. He would venture along a bit, he would see Reggie with the Lewis-gunners. He stumbles his path left round traverse and turn.

At the head of the communication trench, by the white board with the map-reference, the corporal of a Vickers team bent over his brazier of charcoal. He offers an enamelled cup, steaming. Private Ball drank intemperately, as a home animal laps its food, not thanking the kind agent of this proffered thing, but in an eager manner of receiving.

After a while he said: Thank you sergeant—sorry, corporal—very much—sorry—thanks, corporal.

He did not reach the Lewis-gunners nor his friend, for while he yet shared the corporal's tea he heard them calling down the trench.

All of No. 1 section—R. E. fatigue.

He thanked these round their brazier and turned back heavy-hearted to leave that fire so soon, for it is difficult to tell of the

From In Parenthesis

great joy he had of that ruddy-bright, that flameless fire of coals within its pierced basket, white-glowed, and very powerfully hot, where the soldiers sat and warmed themselves and waited to see what the new day might bring for them and him, for he too was one of them, shivering and wretched at the cock-crow.

Give the poor little sod some char[2]—that's what the corporal had said.

No. 1 section were already moving off, he fell in behind, and followed on. Slowly they made progress along the traverses, more easy to negotiate by light of day. Not night-bred fear, nor dark mystification nor lurking unseen snares any longer harassed them, but instead, a penetrating tedium, a boredom that leadened and oppressed, making the spirit quail and tire, took hold of them, as they went to their first fatigue. The untidied squalor of the loveless scene spread far horizontally, imaging unnamed discomfort, sordid and deprived as ill-kept hen-runs that back on sidings on wet weekdays where waste-land meets environs and punctured bins ooze canned-meats discarded, tyres to rot, derelict slow-weathered iron-ware disintegrates between factory-end and nettle-bed. Sewage feeds the high grasses and bald clay-crop bears tins and braces, swollen rat-body turned-turtle to the clear morning.

Men-bundles here and there in ones and twos, in twos and threes; some eating, others very still, knee to chin trussed, confined in small dug concavities, wombed of earth, their rubber-sheets for caul. Others coaxed tiny smouldering fires, balancing precarious mess-tins, anxious-watched to boil. Rain clouds gathered and returned with the day's progression, with the west wind freshening. The south-west wind caught their narrow gullies in enfilade, gusting about every turn of earth-work, lifting dripping ground-sheets, hung to curtain little cubby-holes. All their world shelving, coagulate. Under-earth shorn-up, seeled and propt. Substantial matter guttered and dissolved, sprawled to glaucous insecurity. All sureness metamorphosed, all slippery a place for the children of men, for the fair feet of us to go up and down in.

From Part 4: King Pellam's Launde

It was mild for the time of year, what they call a Green Christmas.

They spoke words of recognition where familiar faces poked out from bivvy-sheets, where eyes peered from dark hovel-holes, flimsy-roofed with corrugated-iron. The gained information, in their passing, of the state of the war as it affected 'A' Company, which brought little additional data to their own observations—it appeared to be equally cushy on the whole half-battalion frontage. They passed a point where the fire-trench cut the pavé road, the road of last night's itinerary. They passed where an angled contrivance of breast-works formed a defensive passage, a cunning opening eastward, opening outward, a sally-way; a place of significance to drawers up of schemes, a pin-point of the front-system known to the Staff. They typed its map reference on their orders in quadruplicate. Brigade clerks had heard of it—operators got it over the wire. Runner Meotti ferreted his way with it, pencilled from a message-pad.

> Officer's party will go out from X 19 a 9 5 AAA will proceed by drain-course left of road to approx. X 19 b 3 2 AAA will investigate area for suspected enemy works at juncture of Sandy and Sally X 19 b 5 2

Barbed entanglements before this place were doubly strong: red-coiled mesh spiked above the parapet, armatured with wooden knife-rest stances.[3]

Here were double sentries and a gas guard. Lewis-gunners squat in a confined dark; there was some attempt at an emplacement. Two of them, industrious, were improving their loophole from the inside, to get a widened field of fire. Grey rain swept down torrentially. The water in the trench-drain ran as fast as stream in Nant Honddu in the early months, when you go to get the milk from Pen-y-Maes.

They turned at a sharp angle, right, where it said:

TO PIONEER KEEP

From In Parenthesis

It was better in the communication trench, where slatters[4] had but lately been at work; and planking, freshly sawn, not yet so walked upon nor mired over, but what its joiner-work could, here and there, make quick that delectation of the mind enjoyed with sight of any common deal, white-pared, newly worked by carpenters. Botched, ill-driven, half-bent-over nail heads protrude, where some transverse-piece jointed the lengthways, four-inch under-timber, marking where unskilled fatigue-man used his hammer awkwardly, marring the fairness of the thing made—also you trip up on the bleeder, very easily.

Since dawn, no artillery of light or heavy, neither ours nor theirs, had fired even a single round within a square kilometre of the front they held. Down on the right they were at it intermittently, and far away north, if you listened carefully, was always the dull toil of The Salient—troubling—like somebody else's war.[5] At least, the veterans, the know-alls, the wiseacres, the Johnnie Walkers, the Mons angels, tugging their moustaches, would incline their heads.

Wipers again.
He can't keep off it—like a bloke with a pimple.
What's the use of the place anyway—where's the sense in it.
Don't talk wet.
Who's talking wet.
You're talking wet.
They get warmed to it—they're well away in
tactics and strategy and
the disciplines of the wars—
like so many Alexanders—are perfect in the great commanders'
names—they use match-ends
to represent
the dispositions of
fosse and countermure.
Who's bin reading *Land and Water*.[6]
Don't nobble Chinese Gordon.
When did they pass you out Hector-boy.
Sheer waste of intelligence—notorious

From Part 4: King Pellam's Launde

example of
the man with the missed vocation.
    G.S.O.1—thet's his ticket—the Little Corporal to a turn—
they're bringing up his baton—wiv the rations.
Wiv knobs on it,
green tabs an' all.
Rose-marie for re-mem-ber-ance.
Green for Intelligence.[7]
Where's yer brass-hat.
Flash yer blue-prints.
Hand him his binocular.
    Keep a civil tongue—knew these parts back in '14—before
yer milked yer mother.
    Not the only bugger—there's Nobby Clark
back at the Transport[8]
reckons he snobbed for 'em at Bloemfontein,
reckons he's a Balaclava baby,
reckons his old par drilled the rookies for
bleedin' Oudenarde,
reckons he'll simply fade away.
They're a milintary house the Clarks—'14,
'14 be buggered—
              Pe-kin
              Lady-smith
              Ashan-tee
              In-ker-man
              Bad-er-jos
Vittoria Ramillies Namur,[9]
thet's the Nobby type o'
battle-honour.

This Dai adjusts his slipping shoulder-straps, wraps close his
misfit outsize greatcoat—he articulates his English with an alien
care.
    My fathers[10] were with the Black Prinse of Wales

[67]

From In Parenthesis

at the passion of
the blind Bohemian king.
They served in these fields,
it is in the histories that you can read it, Corporal—boys
Gower, they were—it is writ down—yes.
   Wot about Methuselum, Taffy?
I was with Abel when his brother found him,
under the green tree.
I built a shit-house for Artaxerxes.^A
I was the spear in Balin's hand
               that made waste King Pellam's land.
I took the smooth stones of the brook,
I was with Saul
playing before him.
I saw him armed like Derfel Gatheren.^B
I the fox-run fire
               consuming in the wheat-lands;
and in the standing wheat in Cantium made some attempt to
form—(between dun August oaks their pied bodies darting)^C
And I the south air, tossed from high projections by his Olifant;
(the arid marcher-slopes echoing—
should they lose
Clere Espaigne la bele).^D
   I am '62 Socrates, my feet are colder than you think
on this
Potidaean duck-board.^E
   I the adder in the little bush
whose hibernation-end
undid,
unmade victorious toil:^F
In ostium fluminis.
At the four actions in regione Linnuis
               by the black waters.
At Bassas in the shallows.
At Cat Coit Celidon.
At Guinnion redoubt, where he carried the Image.

From Part 4: King Pellam's Launde

In urbe Legionis.
By the vallum Antonini, at the place of boundaries, at the toiling estuary and strong flow called Tribruit.
By Agned mountain.
On Badon hill,^G where he bore the Tree.
   I am the Loricated Legions.^H
Helen Camulodunum is ours;
she's the toast of the Rig'ment,
she is in an especial way our Mediatrix.
   She's clement and loving, she's Friday's child, she's loving and giving;
O dulcis
imperatrix.
   Her ample bosom holds:
Pontifex maximus,
Comes Litoris Saxonici,
Comes Britanniarum,
Gwledig,
Bretwalda, as these square-heads say.
   She's the girl with the sparkling eyes,
she's the Bracelet Giver,
she's a regular draw with the labour companies,
whereby
the paved army-paths are hers that grid the island which is her dower.
Elen Luyddawg she is—more she is than
Helen Argive.^I
   My mob digged the outer vallum,
we furnished picquets;
we staked trip-wire as a precaution at
Troy Novaunt.^J
   I saw the blessèd head set under
               that kept the narrow sea inviolate.
To keep the Land,
to give the yield:
   under the White Tower

From In Parenthesis

      I trowelled the inhuming mortar.
   They learned me well the proportions due—
by water
by sand
by slacked lime.
   I drest the cist—
the beneficent artisans knew well how to keep
the king's head to keep
the land inviolate.
   The Bear of the Island: he broke it in his huge pride, and over-reach of his imperium.
The Island Dragon.
The Bull of Battle
   (this is the third woeful uncovering).
Let maimed kings lie—let be
O let the guardian head
keep back—bind savage sails, lock the shield-wall, nourish the sowing.
The War Duke
The Director of Toil—
   he burst the balm-cloth, unbricked the barrow
(cruel feet march because of this
             ungainly men sprawl over us).
O Land!—O Brân lie under.
The chrism'd eye that watches the French-men
that wards under
that keeps us
that brings the furrow-fruit,
keep the land, keep us
keep the islands adjacent.

   I marched, sixty thousand and one thousand marched, because of the brightness of Fflur, because of the keeper of promises
       (we came no more again)
who depleted the Island,
         (and this is the first emigrant host)

From Part 4: King Pellam's Launde

and the land was bare for our going.
   O blessèd head hold the striplings from the narrow sea.
   I marched, sixty thousand marched who marched for Kynan and Elen because of foreign machinations,
      (we came no more again)
who left the land without harness
      (and this is the second emigrant host).
O Brân confound the counsel of the councillors, O blessèd head, hold the striplings from the narrow sea.
   In the baized chamber confuse his tongue:
that Lord Agravaine.
He urges with repulsive lips, he counsels: he nets us into expeditionary war.
   O blessèd head hold the striplings from the narrow sea.
   I knew the smart on Branwen's cheek and the turbulence in Ireland
      (and this was the third grievous blow).^K
   I served Longinus that Dux bat-blind and bent;
the Dandy Xth are my regiment;
who diced
Crown and Mud-hook
under the Tree,
whose Five Sufficient Blossoms
yield for us.
   I kept the boding raven
         from the Dish.
With my long pilum
I beat the crow
from that heavy bough.
   But I held the tunics of these—
I watched them work the terrible embroidery that He put on.
I heard there, sighing for the Feet so shod.
I saw cock-robin gain
      his rosy breast.
I heard Him cry:
      Apples ben ripe in my gardayne

From In Parenthesis

I saw Him die.^L
   I was in Michael's trench when bright Lucifer bulged his primal salient out.
That caused it,
that upset the joy-cart,
and three parts waste.
   You ought to ask: Why,
what is this,
what's the meaning of this.
Because you don't ask,
although the spear-shaft
drips,
there's neither steading—not a roof-tree.^M
   I am the Single Horn thrusting
by night-stream margin
in Helyon.^N
   Cripes-a-mighty-strike-me-stone-cold—you don't say.
   Where's that birth-mark, young 'un.
   Wot the Melchizzydix!—and still fading—jump to it Rotherhithe.

              Never die never die
              Never die never die
              Old soljers never die
              Never die never die
              Old soljers never die they never die
              Never die
              Old soljers never die they
              Simply fade away.¹¹

From Part 7

THE FIVE UNMISTAKABLE MARKS

> *Gododdin I demand thy support.*
> *It is our duty to sing: a meeting*
> *place has been found.*

Invenimus eum in campis silvae
and under every green tree.
Matribus suis dixerunt: ubi est triticum et vinum? Cum
deficerent quasi vulnerati . . . cum exhalarent animas suas in sinu
matrum suarum.[2]

The memory lets escape what is over and above—
as spilled bitterness, unmeasured, poured-out,
and again drenched down—demoniac-pouring:
who grins who pours to fill flood and super-flow insensately,
pint-pot—from milliard-quart measure.

In the Little Hours they sing the Song of Degrees
and of the coals that lie waste.
Soul pass through torrent
and the whole situation is intolerable.[3]

He found him all gone to pieces and not pulling himself together nor making the best of things. When they found him his friends came on him in the secluded fire-bay who miserably wept for the pity of it all and for the things shortly to come to pass and no hills to cover us.

From In Parenthesis

You really can't behave like this in the face of the enemy and you see Cousin Dicky doesn't cry nor any of this nonsense—why, he ate his jam-puff when they came to take Tiger away—and getting an awfully good job in the Indian Civil.

After a while he got his stuff reasonably assembled, and '45 Williams was awfully decent, and wipe every tear, and solidified eau-de-cologne was just the thing so that you couldn't really tell, & doubled along back, with the beginnings of dawn pale on the chalky deep protected way, where it led out to the sunken road, and the rest of the platoon belly-hugged the high embankment going up steep into thin mist at past four o'clock of a fine summer morning.
In regions of air above the trajectory zone, the birds
chattering heard for all the drum-fire,
counter the malice of the engines.

But he made them a little lower than the angels and their inventions are according to right reason even if you don't approve the end to which they proceed; so that there was rectitude even in this, which the mind perceived at this moment of weakest flesh and all the world shrunken to a point of fear that has affinity I suppose, to that state of deprivation predicate of souls forfeit of their final end, who nevertheless know a good thing when they see it.

But four o'clock is an impossible hour in any case.
  They shook out into a single line and each inclined his body to the slope to wait.
And this is the manner of their waiting:
Those happy who had borne the yoke
who kept their peace
and these other in a like condemnation
to the place of a skull.

Immediately behind where Private 25201 Ball pressed his body

From Part 7: The five unmistakable marks

to the earth and the white chalk womb to mother him,
        Colonel Dell presumed to welcome
some other, come out of the brumous morning
at leisure and well-dressed and all at ease
as thriving on the nitrous air.
Well Dell!
   and into it they slide . . . of the admirable salads of Mrs. Curtis-Smythe: they fall for her in Poona, and its worth one's while—but the comrade close next you screamed so after the last salvo that it was impossible to catch any more the burthen of this white-man talk.

And the place of their waiting a long burrow,
in the chalk a cutting, and steep clift—
but all too shallow against his violence.
Like in long-ship, where you flattened face to kelson for the shock-breaking on brittle pavissed free-board, and the gunnel stove, and no care to jettison the dead.

No one to care there for Aneirin Lewis spilled there
who worshipped his ancestors like a Chink
who sleeps in Arthur's lap
who saw Olwen-trefoils some moonlighted night
on precarious slats at Festubert,
on narrow foothold on le Plantin marsh—
more shaved he is to the bare bone than
Yspaddadan Penkawr.
   Properly organised chemists can let make more riving power
than ever Twrch Trwyth;
more blistered he is than painted Troy Towers
and unwholer, limb from limb, than any of them fallen at Catraeth
or on the seaboard-down, by Salisbury,[4]
and no maker to contrive his funerary song.
   And the little Jew lies next him
cries out for Deborah his bride

From In Parenthesis

and offers for stretcher-bearers
           gifts for their pains
and walnut suites in his delirium
           from Grays Inn Road.

              *   *   *

Tunicled functionaries signify and clear-voiced heralds cry and leg it to a safe distance:
leave fairway for the Paladins, and Roland throws a kiss—
they've nabbed his batty for the moppers-up
        and Mr. Jenkins takes them over
and don't bunch on the left
for Christ's sake.

        Riders on pale horses loosed
and vials irreparably broken
an' Wat price bleedin' Glory
Glory
Glory Hallelujah
and the Royal Welsh sing:
Jesu
        lover of me soul . . . to *Aberystwyth*.
But that was on the right with
the genuine Taffies
        but we are rash levied
from Islington and Hackney
and the purlieus of Walworth
flashers from Surbiton
men of the stock of Abraham
from Bromley-by-Bow
Anglo-Welsh from Queens Ferry
rosary-wallahs from Pembrey Dock
lighterman with a Norway darling
from Greenland Stairs[5]
and two lovers from Ebury Bridge,
Bates and Coldpepper

From Part 7: The five unmistakable marks
that men called the Lily-white boys.
Fowler from Harrow and the House who'd lost his way into
this crush who was gotten in a parsonage on a maye.
Dynamite Dawes the old 'un
and Diamond Phelps his batty[6]
from Santiago del Estero
and Bulawayo respectively,
both learned in ballistics
        and wasted on a line-mob.

Of young gentlemen wearing the Flash,
from reputable marcher houses
with mountain-squireen first-borns
prince-pedigreed
from Meirionedd and Cyfeiliog.
C. of E. on enlistment eyes grey with mark above left nipple
probably Goidelic from length of femur.
Heirs also of tin-plate lords
from the Gower peninsula,
detailed from the womb
        to captain Industry
if they dont cop a packet this day
nor grow more wise.
Whereas C.S.M. Tyler was transferred from the West Kents
whose mother sang for him
at Mary-Cray
if he would fret she sang for lullaby:
        We'll go to the Baltic with Charlie Napier
she had that of great uncle Tyler
Eb Tyler, who'd got away with the Inkerman bonus.[7]

Every one of these, stood, separate, upright, above ground,
blinkt to the broad light
risen dry mouthed from the chalk
vivified from the Nullah without commotion
and to distinctly said words,

From In Parenthesis

moved in open order and keeping admirable formation
and at the high-port position[8]
walking in the morning on the flat roof of the world
and some walked delicately
sensible of their particular judgment.

Each one bearing in his body the whole apprehension of that innocent, on the day he saw his brother's votive smoke diffuse and hang to soot the fields of holocaust; neither approved nor ratified nor made acceptable but lighted to everlasting partition. Who under the green tree
had awareness of his dismembering, and deep-bowelled damage; for whom the green tree bore scarlet memorial, and herb and arborage waste.

Skin gone astrictive
        for fear gone out to meet half-way—
bare breast for—
to welcome—who gives a bugger for
the Dolorous Stroke.[9]

But sweet sister death has gone debauched today and stalks on this high ground with strumpet confidence, makes no coy veiling of her appetite but leers from you to me with all her parts discovered.
    By one and one the line gaps, where her fancy will—howsoever they may howl for their virginity
she holds them—who impinge less on space
sink limply to a heap
nourish a lesser category of being
like those other who fructify the land
like Tristram
Lamorak de Galis
Alisand le Orphelin
Beaumains who was youngest
or all of them in shaft-shade

From Part 7: The five unmistakable marks

at strait Thermopylae
or the sweet brothers Balin and Balan
embraced beneath their single monument.
   Jonathan my lovely one
on Gelboe mountain
and the young man Absalom.
White Hart transfixed in his dark lodge.
Peredur of steel arms
and he who with intention took grass of that field to be for him
the Species of Bread.
   Taillefer the maker,
and on the same day,
thirty thousand other ranks.
And in the country of Béarn—Oliver
and all the rest—so many without memento
beneath the tumuli on the high hills
and under the harvest places.[10]

But how intolerably bright the morning is where we who are alive and remain, walk lifted up, carried forward by an effective word.

But red horses now—blare every trump without economy, burn boat and sever every tie every held thing goes west and tethering snapt, bolts unshot and brass doors flung wide and you go forward, foot goes another step further.

The immediate foreground sheers up, tilts toward,
like an high wall falling.
There she breaches black perpendiculars
where the counter-barrage warms to the seventh power where
the Three Children walk under the fair morning
and the Twin Brother[11]
and the high grass soddens through your puttees
and dew asperges the freshly dead.

From In Parenthesis

There doesn't seem a soul about yet surely we walk already near his preserves; there goes old Dawes as large as life and there is Lazarus Cohen like on field-days, he always would have his entrenching-tool-blade-carrier hung low, jogging on his fat arse.

They pass a quite ordinary message about keeping aligned with No. 8.

You drop apprehensively—the sun gone out,
strange airs smite your body
and muck rains straight from heaven
and everlasting doors lift up for '02 Weavel.
    You cant see anything but sheen on drifting particles and you move forward in your private bright cloud like
one assumed
who is borne up by an exterior volition.

You stumble on a bunch of six with Sergeant Quilter getting them out again to the proper interval, and when the chemical thick air dispels you see briefly and with great clearness what kind of a show this is.

The gentle slopes are green to remind you
of South English places, only far wider and flatter spread and grooved and harrowed criss-cross whitely and the disturbed subsoil heaped up albescent.

Across upon this undulated board of verdure chequered bright
when you look to left and right
small, drab, bundled pawns severally make effort
moved in tenuous line
and if you looked behind—the next wave came slowly, as successive surfs creep in to dissipate on flat shore;
and to your front, stretched long laterally,
and receded deeply,
the dark wood.

From Part 7: The five unmistakable marks

And now the gradient runs more flatly toward the separate scarred saplings, where they make fringe for the interior thicket and you take notice.
   There between the thinning uprights
at the margin
straggle tangled oak and flayed sheeny beech-bole, and fragile birch whose silver queenery is draggled and ungraced
and June shoots lopt
and fresh stalks bled
          runs the Jerry trench.
And cork-screw stapled trip-wire
to snare among the briars
and iron warp with bramble weft
with meadow-sweet and lady-smock
for a fair camouflage.

Mr. Jenkins half inclined his head to them—he walked just barely in advance of his platoon and immediately to the left of Private Ball.
   He makes the conventional sign
and there is the deeply inward effort of spent men who would make response for him,
and take it at the double.
He sinks on one knee
and now on the other,
his upper body tilts in rigid inclination
this way and back;
weighted lanyard runs out to full tether,
          swings like a pendulum
          and the clock run down.
Lurched over, jerked iron saucer over titled brow,
clampt unkindly over lip and chin
nor no ventaille to this darkening
          and masked face lifts to grope the air
and so disconsolate;
enfeebled fingering at a paltry strap—

From In Parenthesis

buckle holds,
holds him blind against the morning.
    Then stretch still where weeds pattern the chalk predella—
where it rises to his wire[12]—and Sergeant T. Quilter takes over.

*   *   *

But where's Fatty and Smiler—and this Watcyn boasts he'd seen
the open land beyond the trees, with Jerry coming on in mass—
and they've left Diamond between the beech boles
and old Dawes blaspheming quietly;
and there's John Hales with Wop Costello cross legged under the
sallies, preoccupied with dead lines—gibbering the formulae of
their profession—
Wop defends the D III converted;[13]
and Bates without Coldpepper
digs like a Bunyan muck-raker for his weight of woe.

But it's no good you cant do it with these toy spades, you want
axes, heavy iron for tough anchoring roots, tendoned deep down.
    When someone brought up the Jerry picks it was better, and
you did manage to make some impression. And the next one to
you, where he bends to delve gets it in the middle body. Private
Ball is not instructed, and how could you stay so fast a tide, it
would be difficult with him screaming whenever you move him
ever so little, let alone try with jack-knife to cut clear the
hampering cloth.

The First Field Dressing is futile as frantic seaman's shift bunged
to stoved bulwark, so soon the darking flood percolates and he
dies in your arms.
    And get back to that digging can't yer—
this aint a bloody Wake
            for these dead, who soon will have their dead
for burial clods heaped over.
Nor time for halsing

From Part 7: The five unmistakable marks

nor to clip green wounds
nor weeping Maries bringing anointments
neither any word spoken
nor no decent nor appropriate sowing of this seed
nor remembrance of the harvesting
of the renascent cycle
and return
nor shaving of the head nor ritual incising for these *viriles* under each tree.
   No one sings: Lully lully
for the mate whose blood runs down.[14]
Corposant his signal flare
         makes its slow parabola
where acorn hanging cross-trees tangle
and the leafy tops intersect.
And white faces lie,
(like china saucers tilted run soiling stains half dry, when the moon shines on a scullery-rack and Mr. and Mrs. Billington are asleep upstairs and so's Vi—and any creak frightens you or any twig moving.)

And it's nearing dark when the trench is digged and they brought forward R.E.s who methodically spaced their picket-irons and did their work back and fro, speak low—
cats-cradle tenuous gear.
You can hear their mauls hammering
under the oaks.
   And when they've done the job they file back carrying their implements, and the covering Lewis team withdraws from out in front and the water-party is up at last with half the bottles punctured
and travellers' tales.
Stammer a tale stare-eyed of close shaves,
of outside on the open slope:
Carrying-parties,
runners who hasten singly,

From In Parenthesis

burdened bearers walk with careful feet
to jolt him as little as possible,
bearers of burdens to and from
stumble oftener, notice the lessening light,
and feel their way with more sensitive feet—
you mustn't spill the precious fragments, for perhaps these raw bones live.

   They can cover him again with skin—in their candid coats, in their clinical shrines and parade the miraculi.

   The blinded one with the artificial guts—his morbid neurosis retards the treatment, otherwise he's bonza—and will learn a handicraft.

Nothing is impossible nowadays my dear if only we can get the poor bleeder through the barrage and they take just as much trouble with the ordinary soldiers you know and essential-service academicians can match the natural hue and everything extraordinarily well.

   Give them glass eyes to see
and synthetic spare parts to walk in the Triumphs, without anyone feeling awkward and O, O, O, it's a lovely war[15] with poppies on the up-platform for a perpetual memorial of his body.

Lift gently Dai, gentleness befits his gun-shot wound in the lower bowel—go easy—easee at the slope—and mind him—wait for this one and
slippy—an' twelve inch an' all—beating up for his counter-attack and—that packet on the Aid-Post.

   Lower you lower you—some old cows have malhanded little bleeders for a mother's son.

   Lower you lower you prize Maria Hunt, an' gammy fingered upland Gamalin—down cantcher—low—hands away me ducky—down on hands on hands down and flattened belly and face pressed and curroodle mother earth
she's kind:
Pray her hide you in her deeps

From Part 7: The five unmistakable marks

she's only refuge against
this ferocious pursuer
terribly questing.
Maiden of the digged places
          let our cry come unto thee.
Mam, moder, mother of me
Mother of Christ under the tree
reduce our dimensional vulnerability to the minimum—
cover the spines of us
let us creep back dark-bellied where he can't see
don't let it.
There, there, it can't, won't hurt—nothing
shall harm my beautiful.
   But on its screaming passage
their numbers writ
and stout canvas tatters drop as if they'd salvoed grape to the
mizzen-sheets and the shaped ash grip[16] rocket-sticks out of the
evening sky right back by Bright Trench
and clots and a twisted clout
on the bowed back of the F.O.O. bent to his instrument.
   . . . theirs . . . H.E. . . . fairly, fifty yards to my front . . .
he's bumping the Quadrangle . . . 2025 hours?—thanks—nicely
. . . X 29 b 2 5 . . . 10.5 cm. gun . . . 35 degrees left . . .
he's definitely livening.
   and then the next packet—and Major Knacksbull blames the
unresponsive wire.[17]
   And linesmen go out from his presence to seek, and make
whole with adhesive tape, tweezer the copper with deft hands:
there's a bad break on the Bright Trench line—buzz us when
you're through.

And the storm rises higher
and all who do their business in the valley
do it quickly
and up in the night-shades
where death is closer packed

From In Parenthesis

in the tangled avenues
   fair Balder falleth everywhere
and thunder-besom breakings
bright the wood
and a Golden Bough for
Johnny and Jack
and blasted oaks for Jerry
and shrapnel the swift Jupiter for each expectant tree;
after what hypostases uniting:
withered limbs for the chosen
for the fore-chosen.[18]
Take care the black brush-fall
in the night-rides
where they deploy for the final objective.
   Dark baulks sundered, bear down,
beat down, ahurtle through the fractured growings green,
pile high an heaped diversity.
Brast, break, bough-break the backs of them,
every bone of the white wounded who wait patiently—
looking toward that hope:
for the feet of the carriers long coming
bringing palanquins
to spread worshipful beds for heroes.

You can hear him,
suppliant, under his bowery smother
but who can you get to lift him away
lift him away
a half-platoon can't.
How many mortal men
to bear the Acorn-Sprite—
She's got long Tom
and Major Lillywhite,[19]
     they're jelly-bags with the weight of it:
     and they'll Carry out Deth tomorrow.

From Part 7: The five unmistakable marks

There are indications that the enemy maintains his positions north-east of the central-ride. At 21.35 hrs[20] units concerned will move forward and clear this area of his personnel. There will be adequate artillery support.

And now no view of him whether he makes a sally, no possibility of informed action nor certain knowing whether he gives or turns to stand. No longer light of day on the quick and the dead but blindfold beating the air and tentative step by step deployment of the shades; grope in extended line of platoon through nether glooms concentrically, trapes phantom flares, warily circumambulate malignant miraged obstacles, walk confidently into hard junk. Solid things dissolve, and vapours ape substantiality.

You know the bough hangs low, by your bruised lips and the smart to your cheek bone.
    When the shivered rowan fell
              you couldn't hear the fall of it.
Barrage with counter-barrage shockt
deprive all several sounds of their identity,
    what dark convulsed cacophony
              conditions each disparity
and the trembling woods are vortex for the storm;
through which their bodies grope the mazy charnel-ways—
seek to distinguish men from walking trees and branchy moving like a Birnam copse.
    You sensed him near you just now, but that's more like a nettle to the touch; & on your left Joe Donkin walked, where only weeds stir to the night-gusts if you feel with your hand.

All curbs for fog-walkers, stumble-stones and things set up for the blind, jutments you meet suddenly, dark hidden ills, lurkers who pounce, what takes you unawares, things thrust from behind or upward, low purlins for high chambers, blocks and hard-edged clobber to litter dark entries,

From In Parenthesis

what rides the air
        as broom-stick horrors fly—
clout you suddenly, come on you softly, search to the liver, like Garlon's truncheon that struck invisible.[21]

When they put up a flare, he saw many men's accoutrements medleyed and strewn up so down and service jackets bearing below the shoulder-numerals the peculiar sign of their battalions.
    And many of these shields he had seen knights bear beforehand.
And the severed head of '72 Morgan,
its visage grins like the Cheshire cat
and full grimly.
    It fared under him as the earth had quaked—and the nose-cap pared his heel leather.

Who's these thirty in black harness that you could see in the last flash,
great limbed, and each helmed:
   if you could pass throughout them and beyond
—and fetch away the bloody cloth:
whether I live
whether I die.[22]
But which is front, which way's the way on and where's the corporal and what's this crush and all this shoving you along, and someone shouting rhetorically about remembering your nationality—
    and Jesus Christ—they're coming through the floor,
endthwart and overlong:
Jerry's through on the flank . . . and: Beat it!—
that's what that one said as he ran past:
Bosches back in Strip Trench—it's a
monumental bollocks every time
and but we avoid wisely there is but death.[23]

    Lance-Corporal Bains, sweating on the top line, reckoned he'd

From Part 7: The five unmistakable marks

clicked a cushy get away; but Captain Cadwaladr holds the westward ride, & that's torn it for the dodger. Captain Cadwaladr is come to the breach full of familiar blasphemies. He wants the senior private[24]—the front is half-right and what whore's bastard gave the retire and: Through on the flank my arse.
 Captain Cadwaladr restores
the Excellent Disciplines of the Wars.

And then he might see sometime the battle was driven a bow draught from the castle and sometime it was at the gates of the castle.[25]

And so till midnight and into the ebb-time when the spirit slips lightly from sick men and when it's like no-man's-land between yesterday and tomorrow and material things are but barely integrated and loosely tacked together, at the hour Aunt Woodman died and Leslie's Uncle Bartholomew, and Miss Woolly and Mrs. Evans and anybody you ever heard of and all these here lying begin to die on both parties.

And after a while they again feel forward, and at this time the gunners seemed preoccupied, or to have mislaid their barrage-sheets, or not to be interested, or concerned with affairs of their own; and in the very core and navel of the wood there seemed a vacuum, if you stayed quite still, as though you'd come on ancient stillnesses in his most interior place. And high away and over, above the tree-roofing, indifferent to this harrowing of the woods, trundling projectiles intersect their arcs at the zenith—pass out of hearing, like freighters toil to gradients when you fret wakefully on beds and you guess far destinations.

Down in the under-croft, in the crypt of the wood, clammy drippings percolate—and wide-girth boled the eccentric colonnade, as perilous altar-house for a White Tower, and a cushy place to stuff and garnish and bid him keep him—or any nosy-bloody-Parker who would pry on the mysteries.

From In Parenthesis

    Aisle-ways bunged-up between these columns rising,
these long strangers,
under this vaulting stare upward,
for recumbent princes of his people.
Stone lords coiffed
long-skirted field-grey to straight fold
for a coat-armour
and for a cere-cloth, for men of renown:
Hardrada-corpse for Froggy sepulture.[26]
    And here and there and huddled over, death-halsed to these, a Picton-five-feet-four paragon for the Line,[27] from Newcastle Emlyn or Talgarth in Brycheiniog, lying disordered like discarded garments or crumpled chin to shin-bone like a Lambourne find.

But you seek him alive from bushment and briar—
                       perhaps he's where the hornbeam spreads:
he finds you everywhere.
Where his fiery sickle garners you:
fanged-flash and darkt-fire thrring and thrrung athwart thdrill a Wimshurst pandemonium drill with dynamo druv staccato bark at you like Berthe Krupp's terrier bitch and rattlesnakes for bare legs; sweat you on the sudden like masher Bimp's back-firing No. 3 model for Granny Bodger at 1.30 a.m. rrattle a chatter you like a Vitus neurotic, harrow your vertebrae, bore your brain-pan before you can say Fanny—and comfortably over open sights:
    the gentlemen must be mowed.[28]

And to Private Ball it came as if a rigid beam of great weight flailed about his calves, caught from behind by ballista-baulk let fly or aft-beam slewed to clout gunnel-walker
below below below
    When golden vanities make about,[29]
                   you've got no legs to stand on.
    He thought it disproportionate in its violence considering the fragility of us.

From Part 7: The five unmistakable marks

   The warm fluid percolates between his toes and his left boot fills, as when you tread in a puddle—he crawled away in the opposite direction.

It's difficult with the weight of the rifle.
Leave it—under the oak.
Leave it for a salvage-bloke
let it lie bruised for a monument
dispense the authenticated fragments to the faithful.
It's the thunder-besom for us
it's the bright bough borne
it's the tensioned yew for a Genoese jammed arbalest and a scarlet square for a mounted *mareschal*, it's that county-mob back to back. Majuba mountain and Mons Cherubim and spreaded mats for Sydney Street East, and come to Bisley for a Silver Dish. It's R.S.M. O'Grady says, it's the soldier's best friend if you care for the working parts and let us be 'aving those springs released smartly in Company billets on wet forenoons and clickerty-click and one up the spout and you men must really cultivate the habit of treating this weapon with the very greatest care and there should be a healthy rivalry among you—it should be a matter of very proper pride and
   Marry it man! Marry it!
Cherish her, she's your very own.
   Coax it man coax it—it's delicately and ingeniously made—it's an instrument of precision—it costs us tax-payers, money—I want you men to remember that.
   Fondle it like a granny—talk to it—consider it as you would a friend—and when you ground these arms she's not a rooky's gas-pipe for greenhorns to tarnish.[30]
   You've known her hot and cold.
You would choose her from among many.
You know her by her bias, and by her exact error at 300, and by the deep scar at the small, by the fair flaw in the grain, above the lower sling-swivel—
but leave it under the oak.

From In Parenthesis

Slung so, it swings its full weight. With you going blindly on all paws, it slews its whole length, to hang at your bowed neck like the Mariner's white oblation.

You drag past the four bright stones at the turn of Wood Support.

It is not to be broken on the brown stone under the gracious tree.
It is not to be hidden under your failing body.
Slung so, it troubles your painful crawling like a fugitive's irons.

The trees are very high in the wan signal-beam, for whose slow gyration their wounded boughs seem as malignant limbs, manœuvring for advantage.
The trees of the wood beware each other
                      and under each a man sitting;
their seemly faces as carved in a sardonyx stone; as undiademed princes turn their gracious profiles in a hidden seal, so did these appear, under the changing light.

For that waning you would believe this flaxen head had for its broken pedestal these bent Silurian shoulders.
For the pale flares extinction you don't know if under his close lids, his eye-balls watch you. You would say by the turn of steel at his wide brow he is not of our men where he leans with his open fist in Dai's bosom against the White Stone.[31]

Hung so about, you make between these your close escape.

The secret princes between the leaning trees have diadems given them.
Life the leveller hugs her impudent equality—she may proceed at once to less discriminating zones.

The Queen of the Woods has cut bright boughs of various flowering.

From Part 7: The five unmistakable marks

These knew her influential eyes. Her awarding hands can pluck for each their fragile prize.

She speaks to them according to precedence. She knows what's due to this elect society. She can choose twelve gentle-men. She knows who is most lord between the high trees and on the open down.

Some she gives white berries
        some she gives brown
Emil has a curious crown it's
        made of golden saxifrage.

Fatty wears sweet-briar,
he will reign with her for a thousand years.

For Balder she reaches high to fetch his.

Ulrich smiles for his myrtle wand.

That swine Lillywhite has daisies to his chain—you'd hardly credit it.

She plaits torques of equal splendour for Mr. Jenkins and Billy Crower.

Hansel with Gronwy share dog-violets for a palm, where they lie in serious embrace beneath the twisted tripod.

Siôn gets St. John's Wort—that's fair enough.

Dai Great-coat, she can't find him anywhere—she calls both high and low, she had a very special one for him.[32]

Among this July noblesse she is mindful of December wood—when the trees of the forest beat against each other because of him.

She carries to Aneirin-in-the-nullah a rowan sprig, for the glory of Guenedota.[33] You couldn't hear what she said to him, because she was careful for the Disciplines of the Wars.

At the gate of the wood you try a last adjustment, but slung so, it's an impediment, it's of detriment to your hopes, you had best be rid of it—the sagging webbing and all and what's left of your two fifty—but it were wise to hold on to your mask.

From In Parenthesis

You're clumsy in your feebleness, you implicate your tin-hat rim with the slack sling of it.
   Let it lie for the dews to rust it, or ought you to decently cover the working parts.
   Its dark barrel, where you leave it under the oak, reflects the solemn star that rises urgently from Cliff Trench.
   It's a beautiful doll for us
it's the Last Reputable Arm.
   But leave it—under the oak.
leave it for a Cook's tourist to the Devastated Areas and crawl as far as you can and wait for the bearers.[34]

Mrs. Willy Hartington has learned to draw sheets and so has
Miss Melpomené; and on the south lawns,
men walk in red white and blue
under the cedars
and by every green tree
and beside comfortable waters.
But why dont the bastards come—
Bearers!—stret-cher bear-errs!
or do they divide the spoils at the Aid-Post.[35]
   But how many men do you suppose could bear away a third of us:
drag just a little further—he yet may counter-attack.

Lie still under the oak
next to the Jerry
and Sergeant Jerry Coke.
   The feet of the reserves going up tread level with your forehead; and no word for you; they whisper one with another; pass on, inward;
these latest succours:
green Kimmerii to bear up the war.

Oeth and Annoeth's hosts they were
who in that night grew

From Part 7: The five unmistakable marks

younger men
younger striplings.[36]

The geste says this and the man who was on the field . . . and who wrote the book . . . the man who does not know this has not understood anything.[37]

NOTES TO *IN PARENTHESIS*

General Notes

1. Title-page of Book, *Seinnyessit e gledyf*, etc. See note 2, General Notes, *Y Gododdin*.

2. Quotations on title-pages of each Part. From *Y Gododdin*, early Welsh epical poem attributed to Aneirin (6th century); commemorates raid of 300 Welsh of Gododdin (the territory of the Otadini located near the Firth of Forth) into English kingdom of Deira. Describes the ruin of this 300 in battle at Catraeth (perhaps Catterick in Yorks.). Three men alone escaped death including the poet, who laments his friends. 'Though they may have gone to Churches to do penance their march has for its goal the sure meeting place of death.' He uses most convincing images. 'He who holds a wolf's mane without a club in his hand must needs have a brilliant spirit within his raiment.' There seems an echo of the Empire in the lines I use for Part 1:

    'Men marched; they kept equal step. . . .
    Men marched, they had been nurtured together.'

    Perhaps he had ancestral memories of the garrison at the Wall; of the changing guard of the hobnailed Roman infantry. What seems to be one of the most significant lines I have put on the title-page of this book:

    '*Seinnyessit e gledyf ym penn mameu.*'
    'His sword rang in mothers' heads.'

    The whole poem has special interest for all of us of this Island because it is a monument of that time of obscurity when north Britain was still largely in Celtic possession and the memory of Rome yet potent; when the fate of the Island was as yet undecided. (In Wales, the memory was maintained of *Gwyr y Gogledd*, 'the men of the north'. The founders of certain Welsh princely families came from the district of the Tweed late in the 4th century.) So that the choice of fragments of this poem as 'texts' is not altogether without point in that it connects us with a very ancient unity and mingling of races; with the Island as a corporate inheritance, with the remembrance of Rome as a European unity. The drunken 300 at Catraeth fell as representatives of the Island of Britain.

Notes

The translations are by the late Prof. Edward Anwyl. See his essay *The Book of Aneirin*. Hon. Soc. of Cymmrodorion, Session 1909–10.

3. Pronounce all French place-names as in English.

4. In such words of Welsh derivation as I have used the accent falls on the penultimate syllable.

5. The map on page 62 illustrates the sector described in Parts 3 and 4. It was made by the author for his own convenience when writing Part 3, as an aid to remembering a typical relationship of trenches and roads. It pretends to no accuracy whatever and was roughly copied from a map of much later date than the period of the text. The heavy dotted line indicates the imaginary route taken by the troops in Part 3. The numerals along its length refer to page numbers in the [original printing of the] text. [The map is reproduced from the first edition of *In Parenthesis* (Faber and Faber, 1937).]

Part 3

1. Title. *Starlight order*. Gerard Manley Hopkins, *Bugler's First Communion*, verse 5:
    'March, kind comrade, abreast him,
    Dress his days to a dexterous and starlight order.'
Men went to Catraeth . . . the weak. See General Notes, *Y Gododdin*.

2. *Proceed . . . sings alone*. Cf. Good Friday Office (Rubrics), Roman Rite.

3. *from the small*. Small of butt of rifle.

4. *square-pushing*. From square-pusher, i.e. masher. Term used of anyone of smart appearance when in 'walking-out' dress.

5. *The Wet*. The wet canteen.

6. *night-lines*. Lights used by artillerymen on which to lay gun for night action.

7. *wagon lines*. The horse-lines of an Artillery Unit, some way to rear of gun positions. In the narrative an artillery supply wagon, having delivered its goods at the Battery, is returning to its wagon lines for the night.

8. *Barbara . . . hate*. St. Barbara, the patroness of gunners.

9. *Jac-y-dandi*. Cf. Jack-a-Dandy in Surtees's *Mr. Sponge's Sporting Tour*. *Nos dawch*. Corruption of 'Nos da i chwi'—'goodnight to you'.

10. *little gate . . . that place*. Cf. Malory, book vi, ch. 15.

11. *Jimmy Grove*. In homage to 'Scarlet Town', cf. *Barbara Allen*.

From In Parenthesis

12. *a colder place for my love to wander in.* Cf. English folk song, *The Low Low Lands of Holland*.

    the lengthening light . . . lands. My mother always says, in February, as a proper check to undue optimism:

    > 'As the light lengthens
    > So the cold strengthens.'

13. *festooned slack.* Hanging field telephone wire. See note 18 to p. 43, 'mind the wire'.

    gooseberries. Arrangement of barbed wire hoops, fastened together to form skeleton sphere, the barbs thrusting outward at every angle; usually constructed in trench, at leisure, by day, convenient and ready to handle by night. These could be easily thrown in among existing entanglements.

    picket-irons. Twisted iron stakes used in construction of wire defences.

14. *I want you to play with
    and the stars as well.* Cf. song:

    > 'Loola loola loola loola Bye-bye,
    > I want the moon to play with
    > And the stars to run away with.
    > They'll come if you don't cry.'

15. *caved robbers . . . Maelor.* 'The Red-haired Bandits of Mawddwy' are notorious in local tradition. Historically a band of outlaws who troubled the authorities in mid-Wales in the sixteenth century, about whom legend has accumulated. Perhaps they have become identified with that idea of a mysterious (red?) race lurking in fastnesses which I seem to have heard about elsewhere.

    green girls . . . Croix Barbée. I had in mind Coleridge's *Christabel* and associated her with a nice dog I once saw & a French girl in a sand-bagged farm-building, off the la Bassée–Estaires road.

16. *the cowsons: they've banned 'em.* A complaint against the H.Q. ban on that kind of woollen comforter which covers the ears. These articles of clothing were considered not conducive to general alertness.

17. *cushy.* Used of any easy time, or comfortable place; but primarily of any sector where the enemy was inactive. Habitually used, however, whatever the sector, by the relieved to the relief as they passed each other in trench or on road. These coming from and these going to the front line used almost a liturgy, analogous to the seafaring 'Who are you pray' employed by shipmasters hailing a passing boat. So used we to say: 'Who are you', and the regiment would be named. And again we would say: 'What's it like, mate', and the invariable reply, even in the more turbulent areas, would come: 'Cushy, mate, cushy'.

Notes

18. *mind the wire.* Field-telephone wires, which were a frequent impediment in trench or on roads by night. They ran in the most unexpected fashion and at any height; and, when broken, trailed and caught on any jutting thing, to the great misery of hurrying men.

19. *in wiv the Coldstreams.* It was customary for any new unit going into the trenches for the first time to be attached to more experienced troops for instruction.

20. *shell-case swung.* Empty shell-cases were used as gongs to give gas-alarm. This practice developed into the establishment of Gas Posts and Gas Guards. It was the function of these guards to note the direction of wind, and weather conditions generally and to set up notice, reading, 'Gas Alert', if the conditions were favourable to the use of enemy gas. If gas was actually being put over on the front concerned, the gong was struck, rockets fired, and clappers sounded. False alarms were common, and this weapon, more than any other, created a nervous tension among all ranks. The suspicion of a gong-like sound on the air was often enough to set a whole sector beating brass unwarrantably.

21. *he's got a fixed-rifle on the road.* He, him, his—used by us of the enemy at all times. Cf. Tolstoy, *Tales of Army Life*, 'The Raid', ch. x, footnote: '*He* is a collective noun by which soldiers indicate the enemy.' It was part of the picked rifleman's duty to observe carefully any vulnerable point in or behind enemy trenches (e.g. a latrine entrance, a gap in parapet or between walls, a juncture of paths, any place where men habitually moved, the approach to a stream or pump), and, having taken registering shots by day, to set up a rifle aligned and sighted (i.e. a fixed-rifle) so as to cause embarrassment and restrict movement during those hours which otherwise would have been made secure by the covering darkness. Such points were called 'unhealthy'.

22. *the cleft of the rock . . . hill-country . . . bugger of a time ago.* I mean those caves and hill-shrines where, we are told, the Mystery of the Incarnation was anticipated, e.g. at Chartres; and cf. Luke i. 39: 'And Mary arose in those days, and went into the hill country with haste, into a city of Juda' (A.V.); and there is the association of the moon with the Mother of God.

23. *O.B.L.* 'Old British Line'. In sector here described a dilapidated series of trenches vacated by us in a local advance was so called.

24. *the Disciplines of the Wars.* Cf., as in other places, Shakespeare's *Henry V*. Trench life brought that work pretty constantly to the mind.

From In Parenthesis

25. *hills about Jerusalem.* Cf. Welsh Calvinistic Methodist hymn, the concluding verse of which begins: 'O fryniau Caersalem'.
    David of the White stone. Cf. Welsh song: *Dafydd y Carreg Wen.*

26. *Gretchen Trench.* Name given on English trench maps to German front line trench a little to left of road here described, a continuation of Sandy and Sally Trenches. All German trenches were named by us for convenience.

27. *They've served . . . flares.* Together with various 'traditional song' associations here, I had in mind '*Eddeva pulchra*' and Wace's 'ladies of the land . . . some to seek their husbands, others their fathers'.

28. *This gate . . . whispering.* Cf. Chaucer, *Knight's Tale*. Description of the palace of Mars.

29. *hurdle-stake.* Stout upright of revetting hurdle. Revetment hurdles, or revetting frames, were used to face the earth wall of crumbling breastworks with wire-netting.

30. *china.* From 'china-plate', rhyming slang for 'mate'.

31. *Kitty Kitty . . . in the City.* Cf. music-hall song popular among Field-Telephonists: 'Kitty, Kitty, isn't it a pity in the City you work so hard with your 1, 2, 3, 4, 5, and 6, 7, 8 Gerrard.'

32. *They bend low . . . however so low.* This passage commemorates the peculiar virtues of Battalion Signallers. They were a group of men apart, of singular independence and resource. Excused fatigues, generally speaking, and envied by the ordinary platoon soldier. Accustomed as they were to lonely nocturnal searchings for broken telephone wires, they usually knew the geography of the trenches better than most of us. They tended to a certain clannishness and were suspected of using the mysteries of their trade as a cloak for idling. They also had the reputation of procuring better rations than those served to the platoon and of knowing ways and means of procuring extra comforts—such as officers' whisky, spare blankets, etc. Always, of course, consulted as to any likely new move or turn of events, because of their access to 'the wires'. In general there was legend surrounding them as a body. They were certainly a corporation within the larger life of a Battalion. They seemed to us rather as Ishmaelites to a dweller within the walls.

33. *fire-step.* Raised step in fire-bay about two feet high, formed out of front wall of trench; sometimes built up with layer of sand-bags, sometimes furnished with a duck-board. This last was a good method, it allowed for drainage and afforded a drier seat. The fire-step was the front-

Notes

fighter's couch, bed-board, food-board, card-table, workman's bench, universal shelf, only raised surface on which to set a thing down, above water level. He stood upon it by night to watch the enemy. He sat upon it by day to watch him in a periscope. The nature, height, and repair of fire-steps was of great importance to the front-line soldier, especially before adequate dug-outs became customary in all trenches.

34. *bay*. Fire-bay. The built-out divisions in run of fire-trench. Each bay was connected with the next by a few yards of straight trench. The proportions of this traversing, formed by bay and connecting trench, varied considerably and might be angled square, and exactly and carefully revetted, or be little more than a series of regularly spaced salients in a winding ditch.

35. *Johnson hole*. Large shell-hole, called after Jack Johnson. It is a term associated more with the earlier period of the war; later on one seldom heard it used. It had affinity with that habit of calling Ypres 'Wipers', the use of which by a new-comer might easily elicit: 'What do you know about Wipers—Eeps if you don't mind'. It was held by some that 'Wipers' was only proper in the mouth of a man out before the end of 1915, by others, that the user must have served at the first Battle of Ypres in 1914.

36. *like long-barrow sleepers . . . as Mac Og sleeping*. In this passage I had in mind the persistent Celtic theme of armed sleepers under the mounds, whether they be the fer sídhe or the great Mac Og of Ireland, or Arthur sleeping in Craig-y-Ddinas or in Avalon or among the Eildons in Roxburghshire; or Owen of the Red Hand, or the Sleepers in Cumberland. Plutarch says of our islands: 'An Island in which Cronus is imprisoned with Briareus keeping guard over him as he sleeps; for as they put it, sleep is the bond of Cronus. They add that around him are many deities, his henchmen and attendants' (Plutarch's *De Defectu Oraculorum*; see Rhys, *The Arthurian Legend*). It will be seen that the tumbled undulations and recesses, the static sentries, and the leaning arms that were the Forward Zone, called up easily this abiding myth of our people. Cf. also Blake's description of his picture, 'The Ancient Britons':

'In the last Battle of King Arthur, only Three Britons escaped; these were the Strongest Man, the Beautifullest Man, and the Ugliest Man; these three marched through the field unsubdued, as Gods, and the Sun of Britain set, but shall arise again with tenfold splendour when Arthur shall awake from sleep and resume his dominion over Earth and Ocean.

'. . . Arthur was the name for the Constellation of Arcturus, or Boötes, the Keeper of the North Pole. And all the fables of Arthur and

From In Parenthesis

his round table; of the warlike naked Britons; of Merlin; of Arthur's Conquest of the whole world; of his death or sleep, and promise to return again; of the Druid monuments or temples; of the pavement of Watling-street; of London Stone; of the Caverns in Cornwall, Wales, Derbyshire and Scotland; of the Giants of Ireland and Britain; of the elemental beings called by us by the general name of Fairies; of those three who escaped, namely Beauty, Strength, and Ugliness.' See *The Writings of William Blake*, Descriptive Catalogue.

Compare with note 42, below, 'Pen Nant Govid'.

37. *starving as brass monkeys.* Cf. popular expression among soldiers: 'Enough to freeze the testicles off a brass monkey.'
Diaw! Welsh expletive: Devil, one deprived of light.

38. *dogs of Annwn glast.* According to Lady Guest, writing in the forties of the last century, these baleful animals were still heard by the peasants of Wales, riding the night sky. *Glast* is an obsolete word meaning, apparently, to bark a lot.

39. *parked.* From 'parky' = cold.

40. *fog-smoke wraith they cast a dismal sheen.* Cf. Coleridge, *Ancient Mariner*, part i, verses 13 and 18. This poem was much in my mind during the writing of Part 3.

41. *organisation in depth.* The German trench system as a whole was of greater depth from the front line to the rear defences, of greater complexity and better built than was our own. At least, that was my impression.

42. *Pen Nant Govid . . . night flares.* This whole passage has to do with the frozen regions of the Celtic underworld. At Pen Nant Govid sits that wintry hag, the black sorceress, the daughter of the white sorceress, mentioned in the *Kulhwch ac Olwen*. Again, the Welsh called the chill Caledonian wastes beyond The Wall 'the wild land of hell'. And that theme of the revolving tower of glass in Celtic myth I associate with intense cold and yet with lights shining.

The place of the eight gates where Arthur and his men went, like our Blessed Lord, to harrow hell.

'And before the door of Hell's gates lamps were burning,
when we accompanied Arthur—a brilliant effort,
seven alone did we return. . . .'

The poem attributed to Taliessin from which this fragment is taken is called *Preiddeu Annwn*—'The Harrowing of Hades'. In another place it says:

'Before him no one entered into it. . . .

Notes

And at the harrying of Hades grievously did he sing. . . .
Seven alone did we return. . . .'
and this theme repeats itself at each gate:
'Beyond the Glass Fort they had not seen Arthur's valour. Three score hundred stood on the wall: Hard it is to converse with the sentinel.'

Arthur's descent into Hades is also associated with an attempt to obtain the magic cauldron which would hold the drink of no coward.

We who know Arthur through Romance literature incline to think that the Norman-French genius has woven for us the majestic story of the Table and the Cup, from some meagre traditions associated with a Roman-British leader, who possibly existed historically as a sort of local *dux bellorum*. (Cf. Collingwood and Myres, *Roman Britain and the English Settlements*, ch. xix.) But there is evidence shining through considerable obscurity of a native identification far more solemn and significant than the Romancers dreamed of, and belonging to true, immemorial religion—an Arthur, not as in the bogus print of the seal mentioned in Caxton's preface to Malory: '*Patricius Arthurus Brittanniae, Galliae, Germaniae, Daciae, Imperator*', but rather an Arthur the Protector of the Land, the Leader, the Saviour, the Lord of Order carrying a raid into the place of Chaos.

As C. S. Lewis says of the mediaeval romance makers and their use of Celtic material: 'They have destroyed more magic than they ever invented' (*The Allegory of Love*, p. 27).

43. *third foot for him.* Cf. ninth-century Welsh stanza: 'Mountain snow is on the hill. The wind whistles over the tips of the ash. A third foot to the aged is his staff' (Skene, *Four Ancient Books of Wales*).

44. *little cauldron* and *Joni bach*. Cf. song, *Sospan Fach*, associated with Rugby Football matches; often heard among Welsh troops in France. The refrain runs:

'Sospan fach yn berwi ar y tan,
Sospan fawr yn berwi ar y llawr.
A'r gath wedi crafu Joni bach,'

which implies, I think, that the little saucepan is boiling on the fire, the big saucepan on the floor, and pussy-cat has scratched little Johnny. It is a song of pots, pans, billikins, fire, and a song of calamitous happenings. Mary Ann has hurt her finger, the scullion is not too well, the baby cries in its cradle—it also talks of Dai who goes for a soldier. There is an English version that introduces the words 'Old Fritz took away our only fry-pan'—which lends it more recent associations.[. . .]

45. *the efficacious word.* There was one expletive which, above any other, was considered adequate to ease outraged susceptibilities.

From In Parenthesis

46. *At 350 . . . its bed.* Has reference to adjustment of back-sight leaf for firing at required range. The opposing trench lines were, at this point, separated by approximately 300–350 yards. In other places the distance was very much less. Among the Givenchy craters the length of a cricket pitch, at the most, divided the combatants.

Kinross teeth . . . sixty-three parts properly differentiated. Scotsmen seemed as ubiquitous among Musketry Instructors as they are among ships' engineers. There are 63 parts to the short Lee-Enfield rifle.

47. *Those broad-pinioned . . . white-tailed eagle.* Cf. the Anglo-Saxon poem, *The Battle of Brunanburh*.

where the sea wars against the river. Cf. Dafydd Benfras (thirteenth century), *Elegy to the Sons of Llywelyn the Great*: 'God has caused them to be hidden from us, where the troughs of the sea race, where the sea wars against the great river' (trans. J. Glyn Davies, Cymm. Soc. Transtns., 1912–1913).

Part 4

1. Title. *King Pellam's Launde.* Cf. Malory, book ii, ch. 16.
Like an home-reared . . . piled sods. See General Notes, *Y Gododdin*.

2. *char.* Tea.

3. *knife-rest stances.* Wooden contrivance so shaped, used as framework on which to hang wire entanglement. Characteristically employed to block roads or any place where a portable obstruction was required.

4. *slatters.* Layers or repairers of slats, i.e. the flat pieces of wood which, laid laterally on two parallel lengths of timber, formed a floorboard about 18 in. wide, frequently on wooden supports, so that the space beneath formed a drain, leaving the raised duckboard track dry to walk upon. They were in constant need of repair. They would, in a water-logged trench, become detached and float upon or be submerged in the water, causing considerable inconvenience to any party negotiating the trench, especially by night.

5. *The Salient . . . somebody else's war.* The Ypres salient, 20 miles north of sector here described; always a troubled zone. Any sound of bombardment coming from the north was said to be 'up Ypres way'.

6. *Land and Water.* Periodical well known for articles on strategy, contributed by H. Belloc.

7. *Green for Intelligence.* Green gorget-patches (tabs) were worn by Staff Intelligence Officers.

Notes

8. *back at the Transport.* Transport Lines. A battalion in the trenches left its transport wagons, field kitchens, carpenters, snobs, Quartermaster, Q.M. Sergeants, in the Reserve Area, a few kilometres to the rear.

9. *Pekin . . . Namur.* Cf. battle honours of the 23rd Foot.

10. *My fathers . . . in Helyon.* The long boast in these pages I associate with the boast of Taliessin at the court of Maelgwn: 'I was with my Lord in the highest sphere, on the fall of Lucifer into the depth of hell. I have borne a banner before Alexander, I know the names of the stars from north to south, etc.', and with the boast of Glewlwyd, Arthur's porter, on every first day of May: 'I was heretofore in Caer Se and Asse, in Sach and Salach, in Lotur and Fotor, I have been hitherto in India the great and India the lesser and I was in the battle of Dau Ynyr, when the twelve hostages were brought from Llychlyn, etc.'; and with the boast of the Englishman, Widsith: 'Widsith spoke, unlocked his store of words, he who of all men had wandered through most tribes and peoples throughout the earth. . . . He began then to speak many words . . . so are the singers of men destined to go wandering throughout many lands . . . till all departeth, life and light together: he gaineth glory, and hath under the heavens an honour which passeth not away' (trans. from R. W. Chambers, *Widsith*). I understand that there are similar boasts in other literatures. I was not altogether unmindful of the boast in John viii. 58.

Additional Notes to above passage.

A. *for Artaxerxes.* Cf. the following reported front-area conversation: 'He was carrying two full latrine-buckets. I said: "Hallo, Evan, you've got a pretty bloody job." He said: "Bloody job, what do you mean?" I said it wasn't the kind of work I was particularly keen on myself. He said: "Bloody job—bloody job indeed, the army of Artaxerxes was utterly destroyed for lack of sanitation." '

B. *Derfel Gatheren. Derfel Gadarn*, 'Derfel the Mighty', whose wonder-working effigy, mounted and in arms, stood in the church of Llanderfel in Merionethshire. One of the great foci of devotion in late mediaeval Wales. The Welsh, with engaging optimism and local pride, put aside theological exactness and maintained that Derfel's suffrages could fetch souls from their proper place. In the iconoclasm under T. Cromwell this image was used at Smithfield as fuel for the martyrdom of John Forest, the Greenwich Franciscan. The English made this rhyme of him:

> 'Davy Derfel Gatheren
> As sayeth the Welshmen
> Brought him outlawes out of hell
> Now is com with spear and shield

From In Parenthesis

          For to bren in Smithfield
          For in Wales he may not dwell.'

I quote from memory, and may be inaccurate, but it explains my use of the form 'Gatheren' in text.

C. *in the standing wheat* . . . (. . . *bodies darting*). Cf. Caesar, *Gallic War*, book iv, ch. 32; book v, ch. 17.

D. *And I the south air* . . . *Espaigne la bele.* Cf. *Chanson de Roland*, lines 58 and 59:
               'Asez est mielz qu'il i perdent les testes,
               Que nus perduns clere Espaigne la bele.'
I used Mr. René Hague's translation.

E. *'62 Socrates* . . . *duck-board*. Cf. Plato's *Symposium* (Alcibiades' discourse).

F. *the adder in the little bush* . . . *victorious toil*. Cf. Malory, book xxi, 4.

G. *In ostium fluminis* . . . *Badon hill*. These are the twelve battles of Arthur as given in Nennius's *Historia Brittonum*. Nennius says that at the battle at Guinnion Fort Arthur bore the image of Mary as his sign; and the *Annales Cambriae* records under the year 516: 'Battle of Badon, in which Arthur carried the cross of our Lord Jesus Christ 3 days and 3 nights on his shoulders, and the Britons were victorious.'

H. *Loricated Legions.* In Welsh tradition the Roman armies were so called; it was said that Arthur led 'loricated hosts'.

I. *Helen Camulodunum* . . . *Helen Argive*. This passage commemorates Elen Luyddawg (Helen of the Hosts), who is the focus of much obscure legend. At all events she is associated in some way with wearers of the Imperial Purple; is supposed to be the daughter of Coel Hên, the legendary founder of Colchester; patroness of the 'army-paths': ' & the men of the Island would not have made these great roads save for her'. The leader of armies abroad—a director of men; quasi-historical—so she seems to be discerned, a majestic figure out of the shadows of the last ages in Roman Britain.

J. *Troy Novaunt.* Cf. William Dunbar's poem, *In Honour of the City of London*:
               'Gladdith anon, thou lusty Troy Novaunt.'

K. *I saw the blessèd head* . . . *grievous blow*. There is a fusion of themes here. The predominant and general idea, of the buried king to make fruitful, & to protect, the land—here especially with reference to the head of Brân the Blessed under the White Tower in London. The exhuming of that guardian head by Arthur, who would defend the Land by his own might alone. The repeated spoliation of the Island by means of foreign entanglements and expeditionary forces across the channel—a subject recurring in Welsh tradition, and reflecting, no doubt, the redisposition of troops in the late Roman age, to support the claims of rival candidates to the Purple, and to stem the increasing barbarian pressure at different

Notes

frontiers. The part played by Agravaine toward the climax of the *Morte d'Arthur*. The insult given to Branwen by the Irish, which insult, characteristically caused trouble between the two Islands. See the *Mabinogi* of Branwen, and Lady Guest's notes to that story.

Supplementary Notes to above:

They learned . . . beneficent artisans. The motif employed is from Triad xcii of the third series. When I wrote this passage I was aware of the doubtful nature of my source, but was not fully informed as to its completely spurious character.

The Bear of the Island; The Island Dragon; The Bull of Battle; The War Duke; The Director of Toil. Titles attributable to Arthur.

islands adjacent. i.e. Wight, Anglesey and Man. 'The Island of Britain and the three islands adjacent' is a phrase common in Welsh legend.

keeper of promises. Caswallawn. Cf. the legend of how he led an expedition into Gaul against the Romans to recover a princess called Fflur. He is called 'one of the three faithful ones of the Island of Britain' in the Triads.

that Lord Agravaine. I use Agravaine as a type of the evil counsellor, because his malice was powerful in bringing about the final catastrophe of Camlann. I have not forgotten Mordred nor Gawain; but I see Agravaine as that secondary, urging influence without which the evil thing might not have been brought to fruition.

L. *the Dandy Xth . . . saw Him die.* The Xth Fretensis is, in Italian legend, said to have furnished the escort party at the execution of Our Lord. It will also be remembered that the Standard Bearer of this Legion distinguished himself at the landing of Caesar's first expedition into Kent (Caesar, *Commentaries*, book iv, ch. 25). So that it has in legend double associations for us.

Crown and Mud-hook is another name for 'Crown and Anchor', a game of chance.

terrible embroidery . . . apples ben ripe. Cf. poem, *Quia Amore Langueo*, version given in *Ox. Bk. of Eng. V.*

M. *You ought to ask . . . roof-tree.* Cf. the Welsh *Percivale* story, *Peredur ap Evrawc*: 'Peredur, I greet thee not, seeing that thou dost not merit it. Blind was fate in giving thee favour and fame. When thou wast in the Court of the Lame King, and didst see the youth bearing the streaming spear, from the points of which were drops of blood . . . thou didst not enquire their meaning nor their cause. Hadst thou done so, the King would have been restored to his health and his dominion in peace. Whereas from henceforth he will have to endure battles and conflicts and his knights will perish, and wives will be widowed, and maidens will be left portionless, and all this is because of thee.' See also Jessie Weston, *From Ritual to Romance*, ch. ii.

From In Parenthesis

N. *I am* . . . *Helyon.* 'In the fields of Helyon there is a river called Marah, the water of which Moses struck with his staff, and made the waters sweet, so that Israel might drink. And even in our time, it is said, venomous animals poison that water at the setting sun, so that good animals cannot drink of it, but in the morning, after sunrise, comes the Unicorn, and dips his horn into the stream, driving the Venom from it, so that the good animals can drink there during the day.' (*Itinerarium Joannis de Hese.*)

11. *Where's that birth-mark . . . fade away.* Cf. Hebrews vii. 3, and soldiers' song, *Old Soldiers Never Die*.

Part 7

1. Title. *The five unmistakable marks.* Carroll's *Hunting of the Snark*, Fit the 2nd, verse 15.
   Gododdin I demand . . . been found. See General Notes, *Y Gododdin*.

2. *Invenimus eum.* Cf. Ps. cxxxi. 6, Vulgate (A.V. cxxxii. 6).
   Matribus suis . . . suarum. Cf. Tenebrae for Good Friday, 2nd Lesson of 1st Nocturn. Lamentations ii. 12.

3. *Little Hours . . . intolerable.* The Canonical Hours of Prime, Terce, Sext and None. In the Little Office of the Blessed Virgin Mary (Dominican Rite), the psalms called *Songs of Degrees* are sung, including Ps. cxix, *Ad Dominum*, & Ps. cxxiii, *Nisi Quia Dominus* (A. V. Ps. cxx and Ps. cxxiv). Certain words in the Douay translation influenced this passage.

4. *Arthur's lap.* Cf. Henry V, Act II, Sc. iii.
   Olwen-trefoils. Cf. *Kulhwch ac Olwen*: 'Four white trefoils sprang up wherever she trod'.
   Yspaddaden Penkawr. The Giant task-setter in the *Kulhwch*. 'And Kaw of North Britain came and shaved his beard, skin, and flesh, clean to the very bone from ear to ear. "Art shaved, man?" said Kulhwch. "I am shaved," answered he.'
   Twrch Trwyth. The mysterious destroying beast which is the subject of much of the *Kulhwch* story. He and his brood seem to typify the wrath of the beasts of the earth—and his name stands in Celtic myth like the Behemoth of Job. All Arthur's hosts could not draw him 'with a hook'. As with Leviathan: 'Lay thine hand upon him, remember the battle, do no more.' Lewis Glyn Cothi, a fifteenth-century poet, says of someone: 'He would destroy the towns with wrath, wounds and violence; he would tear down all the towers, like the Twrch Trwyth.'
   Catraeth. See General Notes, *Y Gododdin*.

Notes

seaboard-down, by Salisbury. Refers to Battle of Camlann. Malory, book xxi, ch. 3.

5. *Greenland Stairs.* In Rotherhithe.

6. *his batty.* Interchangeable with 'china' but more definitely used of a most intimate companion. Jonathan was certainly David's 'batty'.

7. *Mary-Cray.* Kentish village on outskirts of London.
   We'll go to the Baltic . . . Inkerman Bonus. Popular song from the period of Napier's Russian expedition:
   > 'We'll go to the Baltic with Charlie Napier
   > And help him to govern the Great Russian Bear.'
   It is the first song I can remember my mother singing me.

8. *the high-port position.* Regulation position at which to hold rifle, with bayonet fixed, when moving toward the enemy. It was held high and slantingly across the body.

9. *Each one . . . and arborage waste . . . Dolorous Stroke.* Cf. Genesis iv; Malory, book xvii, ch. 5; Canon of the Mass, Prayer, 'Quam Oblationem', and Malory, book ii, ch. 15.

10. *shaft-shade.* Cf. Herodotus, book vii, *Polymnia*, Dieneces' speech.
    sweet brothers . . . monument. Cf. Malory, book ii, ch. 19.
    White Hart transfixed. Cf. *Richard II*, Act v, Sc. vi.
    Peredur of steel arms. Peredur. The *Percivale* of the romances called 'of steel arms' in the Triads, and by the Gododdin poet: 'Peredur with arms of steel . . .' (he commemorates other warriors, and proceeds) '. . . though men might have slain them, they too were slayers, none returned to their homes.'
    with intention . . . Species of Bread. In some battle of the Welsh, all reference to which escapes me, a whole army ate grass in token of the Body of the Lord. Also somewhere in the Malory, a single knight feeling himself at the point of death makes this same act.
    Taillefer . . . other ranks. Cf. Wace, *Roman de Rou*: 'Then Taillefer, who sang right well, rode before the duke singing of Carlemaine and of Rollant, of Oliver and the vassals who died at Renchevals.'
    country of Béarn . . . harvest places. Not that Roncesvalles is in the Béarn country, but I associate it with Béarn because, once, looking from a window in Salies-de-Béarn I could see a gap in the hills, which my hostess told me was indeed the pass where Roland fell.

11. *seventh power . . . Three Children . . . Twin Brother.* Cf. Book of Daniel, ch. iii. Here I identify 'The Great Twin Brethren' at the battle of Lake

From In Parenthesis

Regillus with the Second Person of the Blessed Trinity—who walked with the Three Children in the fiery furnace.

12. *chalk predella . . . his wire.* The approach to the German trenches here rose slightly, in low chalk ridges.

13. *D III converted.* Type of Field Telephone.

14. *Lully lully . . . runs down.* Cf. poem:
    'Lully lulley; lully lulley!
    The falcon hath borne my mate away!'

15. *O, O, O, it's a lovely war.* Cf. song, *O it's a lovely war*.

16. *canvas tatters drop . . . shaped ash grip.* The canvas fabric of stretcher. The grip of handles of stretcher.

17. *F.O.O. . . . unresponsive wire.* Forward Observation Officer. An artillery officer having been sent forward to observe effect of our own or enemy fire is reporting to his battery by Field Telephone.

18. *fair Balder . . . fore-chosen.* Here I have associated, in a kind of way, shrapnel with the Thunder God and its effect on the trees of the wood and with the oak-tree as the especial vehicle of the God and with the Balder myth (see *Golden Bough*), and how any chosen thing suffers a kind of piercing and destruction. Cf. Roman Breviary at Sext for the Common of Our Lady, Versicle.

19. *How many mortal men . . . Major Lillywhite.* I mean that the oak spirit, the Dryad, in fact, took these men to herself in the falling tree.

20. *21.35 hrs.* To be said: two one three five hours (9.35 p.m.).

21. *Garlon's . . . invisible.* The knight Garlon who rides invisible, striking where he will, through the pages of the *Morte d'Arthur*.

22. *When . . . whether I die.* Cf. Malory, book iv, ch. 15 (Launcelot at the Chapel Perilous).

23. *and but we avoid wisely there is but death.* King Mark's counsel in the Malory.

24. *He wants the senior private.* In the event of all N.C.O.s being killed or wounded the senior private soldier takes over.

25. *And then . . . castle.* Malory, book x, ch. 29.

26. *Down in the under-croft.* Mordred's siege of the Tower, and memories of the Norman chapel there and Gothic tombs in a dozen churches directed me here.

    Hardrada-corpse . . . sepulture. Cf. the notorious jest of the *hus-carle* to

Notes

Tostig the Earl about the body of Harold H. See *The Heimskringla* History of Harald Hardrade, section 91.

27. *Picton . . . Line.* General Picton was of the opinion that the ideal infantryman was a south Welshman, five feet four inches in height.

28. *the gentlemen must be mowed.* Cf. Somersetshire song: *John Barleycorn*.

29. *golden vanities make about.* Cf. song, *The Golden Vanity*.

30. *county-mob back to back.* The Gloucestershire Regiment, during an action near Alexandria, in 1801, about-turned their rear rank and engaged the enemy back to back.

    Sydney Street East. It is said that in 'The Battle of Sydney Street' under Mr. Churchill's Home Secretaryship mats were spread on the pavement for troops firing from the prone position.

    R.S.M. O'Grady says. Refers to mythological personage figuring in Army exercises, the precise describing of which would be tedious. Anyway these exercises were supposed to foster alertness in dull minds—and were a curious blend of the parlour game and military drill.

    soldier's best friend . . . greenhorns to tarnish. I have employed here only such ideas as were common to the form of speech affected by Instructors in Musketry.

31. *You drag past . . . against the White Stone.* Cf. *Chanson de Roland*, lines 2259–2396, which relate how Roland, knowing that death is near for him, would break his sword on the brown stone, but it will not break, and how among the heaps of dead an enemy watches him, and how he lies by the white stone & the stone of sardonyx, and hides his sword *Durendal* under his body and dies.

32. *Dai Great-coat . . . one for him.* See p. 67 ff.

33. *Among this July noblesse . . . of Guenedota.* The north-west parts of Wales. See Part 4, note 42, 'ein llyw olaf'.

    [David Jones' note ran as follows:
    ein llyw olaf. 'Our last ruler', the last Llywelyn. Killed on December 10th–11th, 1282 near Cefn-y-Bedd in the woods of Buelt; decapitated, his head crowned with ivy. A relic of the Cross was found 'in his breeches pocket'. The greatest English poet of our own time has written:

    > 'And sang within the bloody wood
    > When Agamemnon cried aloud.'

    If the song of birds accompanied Llywelyn's death cry, with that chorus-end, ended the last vestiges of what remained of that order of things which arose out of the Roman eclipse in this Island. 'Ein

From In Parenthesis

llyw olaf' is an appellation charged with much significance, if we care at all to consider ancient things come at last to their term. He belonged, already, before they pierced him, to the dead of Camlann. We venerate him, dead, between the winter oaks. His contemporary, Gruffydd ap yr Ynad Côch, sang of his death: 'The voice of Lamentation is heard in every place . . . the course of nature is changed . . . the trees of the forest furiously rush against each other.']

34. *Cook's tourist to the Devastated Areas . . . for the bearers.* This may appear to be an anachronism, but I remember in 1917 discussing with a friend the possibilities of tourist activity if peace ever came. I remember we went into details and wondered if the unexploded projectile lying near us would go up under a holidaymaker, and how people would stand to be photographed on our parapets. I recall feeling very angry about this, as you do if you think of strangers ever occupying a house you live in, and which has, for you, particular associations.

35. *divide the spoils at the Aid-Post.* The R.A.M.C. was suspected by disgruntled men of the fighting units of purloining articles from the kit of the wounded and the dead. Their regimental initials were commonly interpreted: 'Rob All My Comrades'.

36. *Oeth and Annoeth's hosts . . . striplings.* Cf. Englyn 30 of the *Englynion y Beddeu*, 'The Stanzas of the Graves'. See Rhys, *Origin of the Englyn, Y Cymmrodor*, vol. xviii. Oeth and Annoeth's hosts occur in Welsh tradition as a mysterious body of troops that seem to have some affinity with the Legions. They were said to 'fight as well in the covert as in the open'. Cf. *The Iolo MSS.*

37. *The geste says . . . anything.* Cf. *Chanson de Roland*, lines 2095-8:
'Co dit la geste e cil qui el camp fut,
[Li ber Gilie por qui Deus fait vertuz]
E fist la chartre [el muster de Loüm],
Ki tant ne set, ne l'ad prod entendut.'
I have used Mr. René Hague's translation.

FROM
The Anathemata
TESTE DAVID CVM SIBYLLA

From

PREFACE TO THE ANATHEMATA

'I have made a heap of all that I could find.'[1] So wrote Nennius, or whoever composed the introductory matter to the *Historia Brittonum*. He speaks of an 'inward wound' which was caused by the fear that certain things dear to him 'should be like smoke dissipated'. Further he says, 'not trusting my own learning, which is none at all, but partly from writings and monuments of the ancient inhabitants of Britain, partly from the annals of the Romans and the chronicles of the sacred fathers, Isidore, Hieronymus, Prosper, Eusebius and from the histories of the Scots and Saxons although our enemies . . . I have lispingly put together this . . . about past transactions, [that this material] might not be trodden under foot.'[2]

Well, although this writing is neither a history of the Britons nor a history of any sort, and although my intentions in writing at all could not, I suppose, be more other than were the intentions of Nennius, nevertheless, there is in these two apologies which preface his work something which, in however oblique a fashion, might serve for my apology also.

Part of my task has been to allow myself to be directed by motifs gathered together from such sources as have by accident been available to me and to make a work out of those mixed data.

This, you will say, is, in a sense, the task of any artist in any material, seeing that whatever he makes must necessarily show forth what is his by this or that inheritance.

True, but since, as Joyce is reported to have said, 'practical life or "art" . . . comprehends all our activities from

From **The Anathemata**

boat-building to poetry',[3] the degrees and kinds and complexities of this showing forth of our inheritance must vary to an almost limitless extent:

If one is making a table it is possible that one's relationship to the Battle of Hastings or to the Nicene Creed might have little bearing on the form of the table to be made; but if one is making a sonnet such kinds of relationships become factors of more evident importance.

If one is making a painting of daffodils what is *not* instantly involved? Will it make any difference whether or no we have heard of Persephone or Flora or Blodeuedd?[4]

I am of the opinion that it will make a difference, but would immediately make this reservation: Just as Christians assert that baptism by water 'makes a difference', but that many by desire and without water achieve the benefits of that 'difference', so, without having heard of Flora Dea, there are many who would paint daffodils as though they had invoked her by name.

To continue with these three images, 'which I like', that is, the Battle of Hastings, the Nicene Creed and Flora Dea, and to use them—as counters or symbols merely—of the *kind* of motifs employed in this writing of mine; it is clear that if such-like motifs are one's material, then one is trying to make a shape out of the very things of which one is oneself made; even though, as may well be the case, one may be aware of these things that have made one, by 'desire' only, and not by 'water'—to pursue the analogy used above.

So that to the question: What is this writing about? I answer that it is about one's own 'thing', which *res* is unavoidably part and parcel of the Western Christian *res*, as inherited by a person whose perceptions are totally conditioned and limited by and dependent upon his being indigenous to this island. In this it is necessarily insular; within which insularity there are the further conditionings contingent upon his being a Londoner, of Welsh and English parentage, of Protestant upbringing, of Catholic subscription.

While such biographical accidents are not in themselves any

From Preface to The Anathemata

concern of, or interest to, the reader, they are noted here because they are responsible for most of the content and have had an overruling effect upon the form of this writing. Though linguistically 'English monoglot' accurately describes the writer, owing to the accidents above mentioned certain words, terms and occasionally phrases from the Welsh and Latin languages and a great many concepts and motifs of Welsh and Romanic provenance have become part of the writer's *Realien*, within a kind of Cockney setting. Like the elder boy in *The Prioresses Tale*, who knew well the necessity and significance of the hymn, *Alma Redemptoris Mater*, I too might say:

> 'I can no more expounde in this matere
> I lerne song, I can but smal grammere.'

Seeing that, *as one is so one does*, and that, *making follows being*, it follows that these mixed terms and themes have become part of the making of this writing. But here problems arise and rather grave ones.

The words 'May they rest in peace' and the words 'Whosoever will' might, by some feat of artistry, be so juxtaposed within a context as not only to translate the words 'Requiescant in pace' and 'Quincunque vult' but to evoke the *exact historic over-tones and under-tones* of those Latin words. But should some writer find himself unable by whatever ingenuity of formal arrangement or of contextual allusion to achieve this identity of content and identity of evocation, while changing the language, then he would have no alternative but to use the original form. Such a writer's own deficiency in, or ignorance of, the original language, has only a very limited bearing on the matter, seeing that his duty is to consider only the objective appropriateness of this or that term and its emotive impact within a given context. It is of no consequence to the shape of the work how the workman came by the bits of material he used in making that shape. When the workman is dead the only thing that will matter is the work, objectively considered. Moreover, the workman must be dead to himself while engaged upon the work, otherwise we have that

From The Anathemata

sort of 'self-expression' which is as undesirable in the painter or the writer as in the carpenter, the cantor, the half-back, or the cook. Although all this is fairly clear in principle, I have not found it easy to apply in practice. That is to say I have found it exceptionally hard to decide whether in a given context an 'Whosoever will' is the, so to say, effective sign of a 'Quicunque vult'. Or to give a concrete instance: whether, within its context, my use of the Welsh title 'Gwledig' was avoidable and whether the English translation, 'land-ruler',[5] could have been so conditioned and juxtaposed as to incant what 'Gwledig' incants. The 'grave problems' referred to a few paragraphs back have mostly arisen over questions of this sort. It must be understood that it is not a question of 'translation' or even of 'finding an equivalent word', it is something much more complex. 'Tsar' will mean one thing and 'Caesar' another to the end of time.

When in the Good Friday Office, the Latin, without any warning, is suddenly pierced by the Greek cry *Agios o Theos*, the Greek-speaking Roman Church of the third century becomes almost visibly present to us. So to juxtapose and condition the English words 'O Holy God' as to make them do what this change from Latin to Greek effects within this particular liturgical setting, would not be at all easy. It is problems of this nature that have occupied me a good deal.

With regard to the actual words in the Welsh language I have given the meanings and attempted to give the *approximate* sounds in the notes. Welshmen may smile or be angered at the crudity and amateurishness of these attempts, but something of the sort was necessary, because in some cases a constituent part of the actual form—the assonance—of the writing is affected. I shall give one example of this: I have had occasion to use the word *mamau*. This key-word means 'mothers' and can also mean 'fairies'. Now the Welsh diphthong *au* is pronounced very like the 'ei' diphthong in the English word 'height'. Hence *mamau* can be made to have assonance with the Latin word *nymphae* and the English words 'grey-eyed' and 'dryad', and I have employed these particular correspondences or near correspondences[. . .]

From Preface to The Anathemata

but to the reader unacquainted with the Welsh 'au' sound, the form of this passage would be lost. Over such matters annotation seemed a necessity.

With regard to the Latin terms employed I have noted the liturgical or other contexts. For many readers these notes may appear to be an elucidation of the obvious, but, on the other hand, we are not all equally familiar with the deposits. It is sometimes objected that annotation is pedantic; all things considered in the present instance, the reverse would, I think, be the more true. There have been culture-phases when the maker and the society in which he lived shared an enclosed and common background, where the terms of reference were common to all. It would be an affectation to pretend that such was our situation today. Certainly it would be an absurd affectation in me to suppose that many of the themes I have employed are familiar to all readers, even though they are, without exception, themes derived from our own deposits. When I read in the deposits we have received from ancient Hebrew sources, of Og, king of Bashan, of the Azazel, of Urim and Thummim, I may or may not wish for further information regarding the significance of this ruler, this daemon and this method of divination. Similarly when in my text I have found it necessary to use the words Laverna and Rhiannon, *Dux Britanniarum* and *Ymherawdr*, *groma* and *hudlath*, it is conceivable that some reader may wish for further information about these two goddesses, two titles and two instruments. I have, therefore, glossed the text in order to open up 'unshared backgrounds' (to use an expression coined by Mr C. S. Lewis),[6] if such they are.

The title-page describes this book as 'fragments of an attempted writing' because that is an exact description of it. It had its beginnings in experiments made from time to time between 1938 and 1945. In a sense what was then written is another book. It has been rewritten, large portions excluded, others added, the whole rearranged and considerably changed more than once. I find, for instance, that what is now sheet 166 of my written MS has at different times been sheet 75 and sheet 7.

From The Anathemata

What is now printed represents parts, dislocated attempts, reshuffled and again rewritten intermittently between 1946 and 1951.

The times are late and get later, not by decades but by years and months. This tempo of change, which in the world of affairs and in the physical sciences makes schemes and data out-moded and irrelevant overnight, presents peculiar and phenomenal difficulties to the making of works, and almost insuperable difficulties to the making of certain kinds of works; as when, for one reason or another, the making of those works has been spread over a number of years. The reason is not far to seek. The artist deals wholly in signs. His signs must be valid, that is valid for him and, normally, for the culture that has made him. But there is a time factor affecting these signs. If a requisite now-ness is not present, the sign, valid in itself, is apt to suffer a kind of invalidation. This presents most complicated problems to the artist working outside a reasonably static culture-phase. These and kindred problems have presented themselves to me with a particular clarity and an increasing acuteness. It may be that the kind of thing I have been trying to make is no longer makeable in the kind of way in which I have tried to make it.

In the late nineteen-twenties and early 'thirties among my most immediate friends there used to be discussed something that we christened 'The Break'. We did not discover the phenomenon so described; it had been evident in various ways to various people for perhaps a century; it is now, I suppose, apparent to most. Or at least most now see that in the nineteenth century, Western Man moved across a rubicon which, if as unseen as the 38th Parallel, seems to have been as definitive as the Styx. That much is I think generally appreciated. But it was not the memory-effacing Lethe that was crossed; and consequently, although man has found much to his liking, advantage, and considerable wonderment, he has still retained ineradicable longings for, as it were, the farther shore. The men of the nineteenth century exemplify this at every turn; all the movements betray this if in all kinds of mutually contradictory ways.

From Preface to The Anathemata

We are their inheritors, and in however metamorphosed a manner we share their basic dilemmas. 'And how!' as we citizens of the Old Rome say in our new Byzantine lingo from across the Herring Pond.

When in the 'twenties we spoke of this Break it was always with reference to some manifestation of this dilemma *vis-à-vis* the arts—and of religion also, but only in so far as religion has to do with signs, just as have the arts.

That is to say our Break had reference to something which was affecting the entire world of sacrament and sign. We were not however speculating on, or in any way questioning dogma concerning 'The Sacraments'. On the contrary, such dogma was taken by us for granted—was indeed our point of departure. It was with the corollaries, the implications and the analogies of such dogma that we were concerned. Our speculations under this head were upon how increasingly isolated such dogma had become, owing to the turn civilization had taken, affecting signs in general and the whole notion and concept of sign.

Water is called the 'matter' of the Sacrament of Baptism. Is 'two of hydrogen and one of oxygen' that 'matter'? I suppose so. But what concerns us here is whether the poet can and does so juxtapose and condition within a context the formula H_2O as to evoke 'founts', 'that innocent creature', 'the womb of this devine font', 'the candidates', or for that matter 'the narrows' and 'the siluer sea, Which serues it in the office of a wall, Or as a Moat defensiue to a house'.

A knowledge of the chemical components of this material water should, normally, or if you prefer it, ideally, provide us with further, deeper, and more exciting significances *vis-à-vis* the sacrament of water, and also, for us islanders, whose history is so much of water, with other significances relative to that. In Britain, 'water' is unavoidably very much part of the *materia poetica*. It may be felt that these examples are somewhat far-fetched, but I choose them as illustrations only. And if you consider how the men of some epochs have managed to wed widely separated ideas, and to make odd scraps of newly discovered data

From The Anathemata

subserve immemorial themes (cf. the English Metaphysicals?)[7] my examples may not appear all that strained.

Whether there is a radical incompatibility between the world of the 'myths' and the world of the 'formulae', or whether it is a matter only of historic accident, of an unfortunate and fortuitous association of ideas leading to estrangement and misunderstanding, are questions which are continually debated and discussed at every sort of level by 'thinkers' of all shades of opinion. Clearly such questions are most grave but they do not directly concern us here, nor are they, I think, within our competence. What we are here concerned with and which does fall within our experience and competence, is the effect and consequence of such unresolved elements (whatever the cause) upon the making of works at this present time; the effect, that is to say, upon ourselves, here and now. We are concerned only with the actual existence of a lesion of some sort (whether ephemeral or more enduring we do not know), which appears, in part at least, to be in some way bound up with the historic phenomena indicated. And we are concerned with the present effects of these phenomena only in so far as those effects impinge upon, raise problems relative to, inconvenience or impoverish, handicap the free use of, modify the possibilities of, or in any way affect the *materia poetica*.

The reader may object, with regard to some of the problems cited, suggested or implied throughout this preface, that they exist only for those who adhere to, or hanker after, some theological scheme; or are otherwise entangled in conceptions and images carried over from a past pattern of life and culture. Though it is easy enough to see how such an objection might seem both cogent and convenient, it arises from a serious misinterpretation of the nature of the problems in question. In case my terminology may be thought by some to lend itself to some such misinterpretation I shall attempt a further elucidation, because it is, in my view, very necessary to get this matter clear.

It might not be a bad idea to remind ourselves here that the attitude of the artist is necessarily empirical rather than

From Preface to The Anathemata

speculative. 'Art is a virtue of the practical intelligence.' All 'artistic' problems are, as such, practical problems. You can but cut the suit according to the cloth. For the artist the question is 'Does it?' rather than 'Ought it?'

The problems of which I speak can neither be brought into existence nor made to vanish by your opinions or mine. Though, of course, what we believe, or think we believe, the temper and nature, the validity or otherwise of those beliefs will largely condition our attitude toward all problems. Our beliefs, seeing that they stand in some relationship to the sum of our perceptions, may enhance or lessen our awareness of the very existence of some of those problems. But the problems themselves are inherent in a cultural or civilizational situation, and from problems of such a nature no person of that culture or civilization can escape, least of all the 'poets' of that culture or civilization.

I name the poets in particular, not to round off a phrase, but to state what appears to me to be a fact. The forms and materials which the poet uses, his images and the meanings he would give to those images, his perceptions, what is evoked, invoked or incanted, is in some way or other, to some degree or other, essentially bound up with the particular historic complex to which he, together with each other member of that complex, belongs. But, for the poet, the woof and warp, the texture, feel, ethos, the whole *matière* comprising that complex comprises also, or in part comprises, the actual material of his art. The 'arts' of, e.g., the strategist, the plumber, the philosopher, the physicist, are no doubt, like the art of the poet, conditioned by and reflective of the particular cultural complex to which their practitioners belong, but neither of these four arts, *with respect to their several causes*, can be said to be occupied with the embodiment and expression of the mythus and deposits comprising that cultural complex. Whereas the art of poetry, even in our present civilizational phase, even in our hyper-Alexandrian and megalopolitan situation, is, in some senses, still so occupied.

T. Gilby, in *Barbara Celarent*, writes 'The formal cause is the

From The Anathemata

specific factor that we seek to capture, the mind is a hunter of forms, *venator formarum*'.

This, I suppose, applies to the 'specific factor' that the art of plumbing has as its formal cause, no less than to that which the art of poetry has. But the particular quarry that the mind of the poet seeks to capture is a very elusive beast indeed. Perhaps we can say that the country to be hunted, the habitat of that quarry, where the 'forms' lurk that he's after, will be found to be part of vast, densely wooded, inherited and entailed domains. It is in that 'sacred wood' that the spoor of those 'forms' is to be tracked. The 'specific factor' to be captured will be pungent with the smell of, asperged with the dew of, those thickets. The *venator poeta* cannot escape that tangled brake. It is within such a topography that he will feel forward, from a find to a check, from a check to a view, from a view to a possible kill: in the morning certainly, but also in the lengthening shadows.

Or, to leave analogy and to speak plain: I believe that there is, in the principle that informs the poetic art, a something which cannot be disengaged from the mythus, deposits, *matière*, ethos, whole *res* of which the poet is himself a product.

My guess is that we cannot answer the question 'What is poetry?' (meaning, What is the nature of poetry?) without some involvement in this mythus, deposit, etc.

We know—it goes without saying—that the question 'What is the material of poetry?' cannot be answered without some mention of these same deposits.

We know also, and even more certainly, that this applies to the question 'By what means or agency is poetry?' For one of the efficient causes of which the effect called poetry is a dependant involves the employment of a particular language or languages, and involves that employment at an especially heightened tension. The means or agent is a veritable torcular, squeezing every drain of evocation from the word-forms of that language or languages. And that involves a bagful of mythus before you've said Jack Robinson—or immediately after.

My contention is that all this holds whether the poet practises

From Preface to The Anathemata

his art in some 'bardic' capacity and as a person of defined duties and recognized status in an early and simple phase of a culture (the 'morning' in the analogy employed above) or whether he happens to be a person who, for reasons of one sort or another, 'writes poetry' in a late and complex phase of a phenomenally complex civilization (the 'lengthening shadows' in the analogy) the many amenities of which you and I now enjoy.

We are not here considering the advantages or disadvantages to the art of poetry in these two totally other situations. We are noting only that in the latter situation the causes are *still* linked with the deposits.

We are, in our society of today, very far removed from those culture-phases where the poet was explicitly and by profession the custodian, rememberer, embodier and voice of the mythus, etc., of some contained group of families, or of a tribe, nation, people, cult. But we can, perhaps, diagnose something that appears as a constant in poetry by the following consideration: When rulers seek to impose a new order upon any such group belonging to one or other of those more primitive culture-phases, it is necessary for those rulers to take into account the influence of the poets as recalling something loved and as embodying an ethos inimical to the imposition of that new order. Whether the policy adopted is one of suppression or of some kind of patronage, a recognition of possible danger dictates the policy in either case. Leaving aside such political considerations as may cause such recognition under such circumstances, we may still recognize the 'dangerous' element. Poetry is to be diagnosed as 'dangerous' because it evokes and recalls, is a kind of *anamnesis* of, i.e. is an effective recalling of, something loved. In that sense it is inevitably 'propaganda', in that any real formal expression propagands the reality which caused those forms and their content to be. There are also to be considered the contingent and more remote associations which those forms and their content may evoke. There is a sense in which *Barbara Allen* is many times more 'propagandist' than *Rule Britannia*. The more real the thing, the more it will confound their politics. If the

From The Anathemata

dog-rose moves something in the Englishman at a deeper level than the Union Flag it is not only because of the fragile and peculiar beauty of that flower, but also because the poetry of England, drawing upon the intrinsic qualities of the familiar and common June rose, has, by the single image of a rose, managed to recall and evoke, for the English, a June–England association. The first concept being altogether and undeniably lovely, the other also must be lovely! A very satisfactory conclusion. The magic works. But it might prove most adverse magic to an opponent of the thing, idea or complex of sentiments which the word 'England' is patient of comprising.

The problems that confront the poet, as poet, in any given cultural or civilizational phase, no matter what his subjective attitude toward those problems, and though they concern only such elusive matters as the validity of a word, are themselves as objective as is the development of the aero-engine, the fact that my great-uncle William served in the ranks in the Crimea, that the tree outside the window happens to be an acacia, that field-archaeology has changed some of the accents of, e.g., Biblical criticism, that an extension of state-control characterizes the period in which we now live, or that something analogous to that extension is remarked by students of the period of Valens and Valentinian, and that like effects may possibly have like causes.

The poet is born into a given historic situation and it follows that his problems—i.e. his problems as a poet—will be what might be called 'situational problems'.

If, owing to a complex of causes, sable-hair brushes, chinese white and hot-pressed water-colour paper went off the market, you would, if you were a user of such commodities, be faced with a situational problem of a very awkward but fundamentally material sort. Whatever the consolation of philosophy, no attitude of mind would bring back to your workroom the required commodities which the market no longer provided. You would willy-nilly suffer an inconvenience. The effect of that inconvenience *might* be most salutary, might occasion in you a

From Preface to The Anathemata

most unsuspected inventiveness. Well, the situational problem which concerns us here is of an equally objective nature, but so far from affecting only the materials of one particular kind of artist, it affects man-the-artist as such, and affects him not at one peripheral point, but crucially. Nevertheless, as with the inconvenienced water-colourist, the 'inconveniences' of our situation may turn out to be, in some respects and for some, 'most salutary'. Indeed there is not wanting evidence that such is the case. And so it is that the present situation presents its own particular difficulties with regard to signs in general and the concept of sign.

The whole complex of these difficulties is primarily felt by the sign-maker, the artist, because for him it is an immediate, day by day, factual problem. He has, somehow or other, to lift up valid signs; that is his specific task.

In practice one of his main problems, one of the matters upon which his judgment is exercised ('The virtue of art is to judge') concerns the validity and availability of his images. It is precisely this validity and availability that constitutes his greatest problem in the present culture situation.

If the poet writes 'wood' what are the chances that the Wood of the Cross will be evoked? Should the answer be 'None', then it would seem that an impoverishment of some sort would have to be admitted. It would mean that that particular word could no longer be used with confidence to implement, to call up or to set in motion a whole world of content belonging in a special sense to the mythus of a particular culture and of concepts and realities belonging to mankind as such. This would be true irrespective of our beliefs or disbeliefs. It would remain true even if we were of the opinion that it was high time that the word 'wood' should be dissociated from the mythus and concepts indicated. The arts abhor any loppings off of meanings or emptyings out, any lessening of the totality of connotation, any loss of recession and thickness through.

If the painter makes visual forms, the content of which is chairs or chair-ishness, what are the chances that those who

From The Anathemata

regard his painting will run to meet him with the notions 'seat', 'throne', 'session', *'cathedra'*, 'Scone', 'on-the-right-hand-of-the-Father', in mind? If this haphazard list is, in some of its accidents, yours and mine, it nevertheless serves, *mutatis mutandis*, for Peloponnesians and for Polynesians too.

It is axiomatic that the function of the artist is to make things *sub specie aeternitatis*.

'He said "What's Time? Leave Now for dogs and apes! Man has For ever".'

True, but the works of man, unless they are of 'now' and of 'this place', can have no 'for ever'.

The poet may feel something with regard to Penda the Mercian and nothing with regard to Darius the Mede. In itself that is a limitation, it might be regarded as a disproportion; no matter, there is no help—he must work within the limits of his love. There must be no mugging-up, no 'ought to know' or 'try to feel'; for only what is actually loved and known can be seen *sub specie aeternitatis*. The muse herself is adamant about this: she is indifferent to what the poet may wish he could feel, she cares only for what he in fact feels. In this she differs totally from her sister, the 'Queen of the Moral Virtues', who, fortunately for us, is concerned only with our will and intention.

This applies to poets, artefacturers of *opera* of any sort, at any period of human history. But as I see it, we are today so situated that it is pertinent to ask: What for us *is* patient of being 'actually loved and known', where for us is 'this place', where do we seek or find what is 'ours', what *is* available, what *is* valid as material for our effective signs?

Normally we should not have far to seek: the flowers for the muse's garland would be gathered from the ancestral burial-mound—always and inevitably fecund ground, yielding perennial and familiar blossoms, watered and, maybe, potted, perhaps 'improved', by ourselves. It becomes more difficult when the bulldozers have all but obliterated the mounds, when all that is left of the potting-sheds are the disused hypocausts, and when where was this site and were these foci there is *terra informis*.

From Preface to The Anathemata

To what degree, for instance, is it possible for the 'name' to evoke the 'local habitation' long since gone? I do not raise these questions in order to answer them, for I do not know what the answers may be, but I raise them in order to indicate some of the dilemmas which have been present with me all the time.

When I was a child there was still in vogue the Victorian catch-question 'When is a door not a door?' Today I find that question has gathered to itself unexpected meaning. It has become the keynote of a so to say auto-catechism: When is a door not a door? When is a sign not a sign? When is what was valid no longer valid?

Such questions and attempts to answer them are in part reflected in the preoccupation with the 'abstract' in the visual arts. This preoccupation, whether mistaken or rewarding, is neither whim nor accident but is determined by historic causes affecting all this whole business of sign and what is signified, now-ness and place-ness and loves and validities of many sorts and kinds.

What goes for tinker goes for tailor; and it is worth noting, for again it is not accidental, that the man who was super-sensitive to the unique and specific possibilities and demands of his own art, should have shown in his attitude toward that art and in that art itself, how analogous are some of the problems that the muse sets for the writer and those she sets for the painter. And further that this artist, while pre-eminently 'contemporary' and indeed 'of the future', was also of all artists the most of site and place. And as for 'the past', as for 'history', it was from the ancestral mound that he fetched his best garlands and Clio ran with him a lot of the way—if under the name of Brigit. So that although most authentically the bard of the shapeless cosmopolis and of the megalopolitan diaspora, he could say

> 'Come ant daunce wyt me
> In Irelaunde'.

In taking Joyce to illustrate the problem I do so because any problem inherent in the arts today, and in particular in that of

From The Anathemata

writing, is illuminated by so doing. Quite irrespective of whether we approve or deprecate his matter or his form or both, Joyce was centrally occupied with the formal problems of art, as exemplified in a particular art and in his own very particular deployment of that art. It is just such *kinds* of artist who alone illustrate the artistic dilemmas of any age. Hopkins, 'as one born out of due time', but before his time (yet how very much *of* his time!), was just such another. And we know how he, Manley Hopkins, stands over so many later artists, saying, in the words of another and pre-eminent living artist,

'And I Tiresias have foresuffered all'.

And Browning too might well have his say and continue the quotation,

'Enacted on this same divan or bed'.

That bed may indeed seem procrustean, for the artist may be stretched upon it

'Dead from the waist down'

and it is on such a couch that the muse exacts and interrogates, subsequent to

'The fine delight that fathers thought'.

To take an example from a visual art: Though our presiding spirit were akin to that which presided over the illustrative charm of Beatrix Potter, we should be more than foolish to close our eyes to the existence of Pablo Picasso, because our problems as a visual artist would be bound in some way or other, to some degree or other, to involve matters over which that Spanish Hercules has laboured in more than twelve modes. Behind his untiring inventiveness there is the desire to uncover a valid sign. And that desire is, as I have said, incumbent upon all who practise an art.

A rhyme I associate with St Thomas More (but perhaps it is not his) runs

From Preface to The Anathemata

'The cook that doth to painting fall
I ween he shall prove a fool'.

In practice maybe—it all depends. But in idea he will not be proved so foolish as the painter who thinks cookery not subject to the same demands of the muse as is painting or any making that contrives things patient of being 'set up to the gods'.

The foregoing considerations may appear to lack continuity and to run tangent, but they will perhaps indicate something of my attitude toward human works of all sorts and are thus not out of place in an introduction to this attempted sort of work of my own.

I call what I have written *The Anathemata*. (The dictionary puts the accent on the *third* syllable in contradistinction to 'anathemas'.)

It came to have this title in the following way: I knew that in antiquity the Greek word *anathema* (spelt with an epsilon) meant (firstly) something holy but that in the N.T. it is restricted to the opposite sense. While this duality exactly fitted my requirements, the English word 'anathemas', because referring only to that opposite sense, was of no use to me. I recalled, however, that there was the other English plural, 'anathemata', meaning devoted things, and used by some English writers down the centuries, thus preserving in our language the ancient and beneficent meaning; for 'anathemata' comes from *anathema* spelt with an eta, of which the epsilon form is a variant.

It might be said that 'anathemata' precludes 'anathemas' no less than *vice versa*, but considering that the former carries us back to a beneficent original, and the latter only to a particular meaning of a variant of that original, I decided that 'anathemata' would serve my double purpose, even if it did so only by means of a pun.

Subsequent to deciding upon this title, I noted that in a reference to St John Chrysostom it was said that he described the word as 'things . . . laid up from other things'. And again that in Homer it refers only to delightful things and to ornaments. And

From The Anathemata

further, that it is a word having certain affinities with *agalma*, meaning what is glorious, and so used of statue, image, figure. (Hence our word figure-stone, agalmatolite, called also pagodite because the sacred images or pagodas of Asia are carved in it.) And again in the gospel, after narrating the incident of the widow's mite, St Luke speaks of the onlookers who admired the 'goodly stones and gifts' that embellished the temple and he uses the word 'anathemata' of those gifts. And in the middle of the last century, an author, commenting on ancient votive offerings—figurines of animals—writes of 'such anathemata being offered by the poor'.

So I mean by my title as much as it can be made to mean, or can evoke or suggest, however obliquely: the blessed things that have taken on what is cursed and the profane things that somehow are redeemed: the delights and also the 'ornaments', both in the primary sense of gear and paraphernalia and in the sense of what simply adorns; the donated and votive things, the things dedicated after whatever fashion, the things in some sense made separate, being 'laid up from other things'; things, or some aspect of them, that partake of the extra-utile and of the gratuitous; things that are the signs of something other, together with those signs that not only have the nature of a sign, but are themselves, under some mode, what they signify. Things set up, lifted up, or in whatever manner made over to the gods.

But here I shall have to recall an ancient distinction as it very much concerns, and is mixed up with, what I include under anathemata.

It is spoken of under the terms *prudentia* and *ars*. With regard to the latter, the 'virtue of art', a compact or shipshape passage occurs in a recent book.[8] This passage concludes thus: 'The emphasis is on the thing to be done, not, as in the moral virtues, on our personal dispositions in doing it.' The one is concerned only for our intentions and dispositions, and the other only for the formal dispositions that comprise an artefact. One cares for us and our final condition, the other for the work and *its* final condition. Our final condition or last end is not yet, whereas our

From Preface to The Anathemata

artefacts have their completion now or never. For which reason, while Prudentia is exercised about our intentions, Ars is concerned with the shape of a finished article. She *cannot*, as the other *must*, wait till the Judgment.

The distinction could hardly be greater in all respects—that is what makes the analogies particularly significant. For it emerges that both are concerned with the proper integration and perfection of a shape, in the one case that of persons and in the other of perishable things. Both then are concerned with what is patient of being 'devoted', 'laid up from other things', 'consecrated to divine use', made anathemata in some sense or other.

So that at one end of the scale or Jacob's ladder or song of degrees, we can include, in respect of things offered, those differing coloured marks or spots that boys chalk carefully on their whipping-tops,[9] which, when they whip the top, take on definity and form and appear as revolving circles of rainbow hue. (And if this is not a gift to the muse, then I do not know what is, and a falsity pervades my suppositions and analogies throughout.)

At the other end we can include that which comprises anathemata in *every possible* sense, offerings of both persons and things, including those things over which the minister is directed to say '. . . bless, ascribe to, ratify, make reasonable and acceptable'.[10]

We note that he is not directed to say those words with reference to grapes and wheat,[11] but with reference to things which have already passed under the jurisdiction of the muse, being themselves quasi-artefacts, made according to a *recta ratio* and involving the operation of several arts, as that of the mill, the kneading-board, the oven, the *torcular*, the vat.

So that, leaving aside much else, we could not have the bare and absolute essentials wherewith to obey the command 'Do this for a recalling[12] of me', without artefacture. And where artefacture is there is the muse, and those cannot escape her presence who with whatever intention employ the signs of wine and bread. Something has to be made by us before it can become for us his sign who made us. This point he settled in the upper

From The Anathemata

room. No artefacture no Christian religion.[13] Thus far what goes for Mass-house goes for Meeting-house.[14] The muse then is with us all the way—she that has music wherever she goes.

This leads direct to a further point. I have already referred to what this writing 'is about'; but I now wish to add something rather more particularized and somewhat difficult to say.

In a sense the fragments that compose this book are about, or around and about, matters of all sorts which, by a kind of quasi-free association, are apt to stir in my mind at any time and as often as not 'in the time of the Mass'. The mental associations, liaisons, meanderings to and fro, 'ambivalences', asides, sprawl of the pattern, if pattern there is—these thought-trains (or, some might reasonably say, trains of distraction and inadvertence) have been as often as not initially set in motion, shunted or buffered into near sidings or off to far destinations, by some action or word, something seen or heard, during the liturgy. The speed of light, they say, is very rapid—but it is nothing to the agility of thought and its ability to twist and double on its tracks, penetrate recesses and generally nose about. You can go around the world and back again, in and out the meanders, down the history-paths, survey *religio* and *superstitio*, call back many yesterdays, but yesterday week ago, or long, long ago, note Miss Weston's last year's Lutetian trimmings and the Roman laticlave on the deacon's Dalmatian tunic, and a lot besides, during those few seconds taken by the presbyter to move from the Epistle to the Gospel side, or while he leans to kiss the board or stone (where are the tokens of the departed) or when he turns to incite the living *plebs* to assist him.

But if the twists and turns that comprise thought are quicker than light, the action of making anything—any artefact or work of any sort—from those thoughts, is, as the tag says, longer.

The mote of dust or small insect seen for an instant in a bend or pale of light, may remind us of the bird that winged swiftly through the lighted mote-hall, and that I suppose cannot but remind us of the northern Witan and that may recall the city of York and that again Canterbury and that the 'blisful briddes', and

From Preface to The Anathemata

that Tabard Street, E.C.1, and that London Bridge, and that the South Bank and its present abstract artefacts, and that again Battersea, and that the forcing of the river at the Claudian invasion, and that the 'Battersea shield', and that that other abstract art of the La Tène Celts in the British Museum in Bloomsbury, W.C.1.

This much and much more can be 'thought of' in a second or so. But suppose you had to make the actual journey by London Transport and British Railways, starting from the station down the road (Harrow Met.), keeping strictly to the order of your mental itinerary. It would take you not seconds but many, many hours; I should want some days and a long rest.

Now making a work is not thinking thoughts but accomplishing an actual journey. There are the same tediums: strugglings with awkward shapes that won't fit into the bag, the same mislayings, as of tickets, the missings of connections, the long waits, the misdirections, the packing of this that you don't need and the forgetting of that which you do, and all such botherations, not to speak of more serious mishaps. Until in the end you may perhaps wish you had never observed that mote of dust in the beam from the clerestory light that set you willy-nilly on your journey. You might have been better occupied. You well might. It is not without many such misgivings that I write this introduction to the meanderings that comprise this book.

What I have written has no plan, or at least is not planned. If it has a shape it is chiefly that it returns to its beginning. It has themes and a theme even if it wanders far. If it has a unity it is that what goes before conditions what comes after and *vice versa*. Rather as in a longish conversation between two friends, where one thing leads to another; but should a third party hear fragments of it, he might not know how the talk had passed from the cultivation of cabbages to Melchizedek, king of Salem. Though indeed he might guess.

Which means, I fear, that you won't make much sense of one bit unless you read the lot.

My intention has not been to 'edify' (in the secondary but

From The Anathemata

accepted and customary sense of that word), nor, I think, to persuade, but there is indeed an intention to 'uncover'; which is what a 'mystery' does, for though at root 'mystery' implies a closing, all 'mysteries' are meant to disclose, to show forth something. So that in one sense it *is* meant to 'edify', i.e. 'to set up'. Otherwise my intentions would not sort very well with the title of my book, *The Anathemata*, 'the things set up, etc.'

Most of all, perhaps, I could wish of my 'mystery', *misterium* or *ministerium*, that it should give some kind of 'pleasure', for I believe in Poussin's dictum: 'The goal of painting is delight', and as I have already said, it is one of my few convictions that what goes for one art goes for all of 'em, in some sense or other.

To reinforce something already touched upon: I regard my book more as a series of fragments, fragmented bits, chance scraps really, of records of things, vestiges of sorts and kinds of *disciplinae*,[15] that have come my way by this channel or that influence. Pieces of stuffs that happen to mean something to me and which I see as perhaps making a kind of coat of many colours, such as belonged to 'that dreamer' in the Hebrew myth.[16] Things to which I would give a related form, just as one does in painting a picture. You use the things that are yours to use because they happen to be lying about the place or site or lying within the orbit of your 'tradition'. It is very desirable in the arts to know the meaning of the word ex-orbitant, or there is pastiche or worse.

Of course, in any case, there may well be pastiche, padding, things not gestant and superficialities of all sorts; but all this is inevitable if you get outside what I believe Blake called the artist's horizon. I have tried to keep inside it. Necessarily within that 'horizon' you will find material of which it could be said

> '. . . in scole is gret altercacioun
> In this matere, and gret disputision'

and, although it is absolutely incumbent upon the artist to use this disputed 'matere', he may be the least qualified to discuss

From Preface to The Anathemata

it, nor is it his business, *qua* artist. He has not infrequently to say, quoting from the same clear source of Englishness,

> 'Those been the cokkes wordes and not myne'.

Rather than being a seer or endowed with the gift of prophecy he is something of a vicar whose job is legatine—a kind of Servus Servorum to deliver what has been delivered to him, who can neither add to nor take from the deposits. It is not that that we mean by 'originality'. There is only one tale to tell even though the telling is patient of endless development and ingenuity and can take on a million variant forms. I imagine something of this sort to be implicit in what Picasso is reported as saying: 'I do not seek, I find'.

I intend what I have written to be said. While marks of punctuation, breaks of line, lengths of line, grouping of words or sentences and variations of spacing are visual contrivances they have here an aural and oral intention. You can't get the intended meaning unless you hear the sound and you can't get the sound unless you observe the score; and pause-marks on a score are of particular importance. Lastly, it is meant to be said with deliberation—slowly as opposed to quickly—but 'with deliberation' is the best rubric for each page, each sentence, each word.

I would especially emphasize this point, for what I have written will certainly lose half what I intend, indeed, it will fail altogether, unless the advice 'with deliberation' is heeded. Each word is meant to do its own work, but each word cannot do its work unless it is given due attention. It was written to be read in that way. And, as I say above, the spacings are of functional importance; they are not there to make the page look attractive—though it would be a good thing should that result also.

✝

PARENTIBVS
MEIS·ET·PRIOR
IBVS·EORVM
ET·OMNIBVS
INDIGENIS
OMNIS·CAN
DIDAE·INSVLAE
BRITTONVM
GENTIS

From I

RITE AND FORE-TIME

We already and first of all discern him making this thing other. His groping syntax, if we attend, already shapes:
 ADSCRIPTAM, RATAM, RATIONABILEM . . .[1] and by pre-application and for *them*, under modes and patterns altogether theirs, the holy and venerable hands[2] lift up an efficacious sign.

These, at the sagging end and chapter's close, standing humbly before the tables spread, in the apsidal houses, who intend life:
    between the sterile ornaments
    under the pasteboard baldachins
as, in the young-time, in the sap-years:
    between the living floriations
    under the leaping arches.

    (Ossific, trussed with ferric rods, the failing numina of column and entablature, the genii of spire and triforium, like great rivals met when all is done, nod recognition across the cramped repeats of their dead selves.)

These rear-guard details in their quaint attire, heedless of incongruity, unconscious that the flanks are turned and all connecting files withdrawn or liquidated—that dead symbols litter to the base of the cult-stone, that the stem by the palled stone is thirsty, that the stream is very low.

From The Anathemata

    The utile infiltration nowhere held
      creeps vestibule
is already at the closed lattices,[3] is coming through each door.

The cult-man stands alone in Pellam's[4] land: more precariously than he knows he guards the *signa*: the pontifex among his house-treasures (the twin-*urbes* his house is), he can fetch things new and old:[5] the tokens, the matrices, the institutes, the ancilia, the fertile ashes—the palladic foreshadowings: the things come down from heaven together with the kept memorials, the things lifted up and the venerated trinkets.

This man, so late in time, curiously surviving, shows courtesy to the objects when he moves among, handles or puts aside the name-bearing instruments, when he shows every day in his hand[6] the salted cake given for this *gens* to savour all the *gentes*.[7]

    Within the railed tumulus[8]
        he sings high and he sings low.

    In a low voice
        as one who speaks
where a few are, gathered in high-room
    and one, gone out.

    There's conspiracy here:
      Here is birthday and anniversary, if there's continuity here, there's a new beginning.
      By intercalation of weeks
          (since the pigeons were unfledged
        and the lambs still young)
        they've adjusted the term
        till this appointed night
                   (Sherthursdaye bright)[9]
        the night that falls
        when she's first at the full

From I: Rite and Fore-Time

   after the vernal turn
   when in the Ram he runs.[10]

By the two that follow Aquarius[11]
toiling the dry meander:
        through the byes
   under the low porch
   up the turning stair
   to the high nave

        where the board is
   to spread the board-cloth
   under where the central staple is
   for the ritual light.

 In the high cave they prepare
        for guest to be the *hostia*.
They set the thwart-boards
and along:
   Two for the Gospel-makers[12]
   One for the other Son of Thunder
   One for the swordsman, at the right-board,[13] after;
to make him feel afloat. One for the man from Kerioth,[14] seven for the rest in order.

They besom here and arrange this handy, tidy here, and furbish with the green of the year the cross-beams and the gleaming board.

 They make all shipshape
   for she must be trim
        dressed and gaudeous
   all Bristol-fashion here
   for:
        Who d'you think is Master of her?

From The Anathemata

In the prepared high-room
he implements inside time and late in time under forms indelibly
marked by locale and incidence, deliberations made out of time,
before all oreogenesis

       on this hill
  at a time's turn
         not on any hill
  but on this hill.

            *   *   *

At this unabiding Omphalos
    this other laughless rock
at the stone of division
    above the middle water-deeps[15]
at the turn of time
    not at any time, but
at this acceptable time.
From the year of
    the lord-out-of-Ur
about two millennia.
Two thousand lents again
    since the first barley mow.[16]
Twenty millennia (and what millennia more?)
Since he became
    man master-of-plastic.[17]

Who were his *gens*-men or had he no *Hausname* yet
no *nomen* for his *fecit*-mark
    the Master of the Venus?
whose man-hands god-handled the Willendorf stone
    before they unbound the last glaciation
for the Uhland Father to be-ribbon *die blaue Donau*
    with his Vanabride blue.[18]
O long before they lateen'd her Ister
or Romanitas manned her gender'd stream.

From I: Rite and Fore-Time

O Europa!
                                     how long and long and long and very long again, before you'll maze the waltz-forms in gay Vindobona in the ramshackle last phases; or god-shape the modal rhythms for nocturns in Melk in the young-time;[19] or plot the Rhaetian limits in the Years of the City.[20]
        But already he's at it
the form-making proto-maker
busy at the fecund image of her.

                Chthonic? why yes
but mother of us.
    Then it is these abundant *ubera*, here, under the species of worked lime-rock, that gave suck to the lord? She that they already venerate (what other could they?)
                her we declare?
Who else?[21]
                And see how they run, the juxtaposed forms, brighting the vaults of Lascaux; how the linear is wedded to volume, how they do, within, in an unbloody manner, under the forms of brown haematite and black manganese on the graved lime-face, what is done, without,
                far on the windy tundra
at the kill
that the kindred may have life.
                O God!
O the Academies!

What ages since
his other marvel-day
                when times turned?
and *how* turned!
When

From The Anathemata

(How?
    from early knocking stick or stane?)
the first New Fire wormed
    at the Easter of Technics.
What a holy Saturn's day!
O vere beata nox![22]

    A hundred thousand equinoxes
(less or more)
since they cupped the ritual stones
for the faithful departed.[23]

    What, from this one's cranial data, is like to have been his kindred's psyche; in that they, along with the journey-food, donated the votive horn? and with what *pietas* did they donate these among the dead—the life-givers—and by what rubric?
Was their oral gloss from a Heidelberg gaffer or did they emend a Piltdown use, was the girl from Lime Street a butty of theirs, or were the eight Carmel fathers consanguine or of any affinity to those that fathered them, that told what they had heard with their ears of those german to them, before the palmy arbours began again to pine—and at which of the boreal oscillations?
    And before them?
those who put on their coats to oblate the things set apart in an older Great Cold.
    And who learned them
if not those whose fathers had received or aped the groping *disciplina* of their cognates, or lost or found co-laterals, on the proto-routes or at the lithic foci?
    Tundra-wanderers?
or was there no tundra as yet, or not as yet again, to wander—but grew green the rashes over again? Or was all once again *informis*, that Cronos for the third time might see how his lemmings run and hear the cry of his tailless hare from south of the sixties, from into the forties?

From I: Rite and Fore-Time

                For the phases and phase-groups
sway toward and fro within that belt of latitude.
There's where the world's a stage
                for transformed scenes
with metamorphosed properties
                      for each shifted set.
Now naked as an imagined *belle sauvage,* or as is the actual Mirriam.[24]
Now shirted, kilted, cloaked, capped and shod, as were the five men of Jutland, discovered in their peaty cerements, or as the bear-coped Gilyak is, or was, the other day.

The mimes deploy:
                anthropoid
                anthropoi.
Who knows at what precise phase, or from what floriate greenroom, the Master of Harlequinade, himself not made, maker of sequence and permutation in all things made, called us from our co-laterals out, to dance the Funeral Games of the Great Mammalia, as, long, long, long before, these danced out the Dinosaur?

Now, from the draughty flats
                      the ageless cherubs
pout the Southerlies.
Now, Januarius brings in the millennial snow that makes the antlered mummers glow for many a hemera.
                    The *Vorzeit*-masque is on
that moves to the cosmic introit.
Col canto the piping for this turn.
Unmeasured, irregular in stress and interval, of interior rhythm, modal.
                If tonic and final are fire
the dominant is ice
                if fifth the fire
the cadence ice.

From The Anathemata

At these Nocturns the hebdomadary is apt to be vested for five hundred thousand weeks.[25]
Intunes the Dog:
    Benedicite, ignis . . .
Cantor Notus and Favonius with all their south-aisled numina:
    con flora cálida
    mit warmer Fauna
The Respond is with the Bear:
    Benedicite, frigus . . .
Super-pellissed, stalled in crystallos, from the gospel-side, choir all the boreal schola
    mit kalter Flora
    con fauna fria
Now, sewn fibre is superfluous where Thames falls into Rhine. Now they would be trappers of every tined creature and make corners in ulotrichous hide and establish their wool-cartels as south as Los Millares. Where the stones shall speak of his cupola-makers:[26] but here we speak of long, long before their time.
    When is Tellus
to give her dear fosterling
    her adaptable, rational, elect
and plucked-out otherling
    a reasonable chance?
Not yet—but soon, very soon
    as lithic phases go.

So before then?
    Did the fathers of those
who forefathered them
    (if by genital or ideate begetting)
set apart, make other, oblate?

By what rote, if at all
  had they the suffrage:
    Ascribe to, ratify, approve

From I: Rite and Fore-Time

in the humid paradises
       of the Third Age?[27]
But who or what, before these?
       Had they so far to reach the ground?
and what of the pelvic inclination of their co-laterals, whose far cognates went—on how many feet?—in the old time before them?
For all WHOSE WORKS FOLLOW THEM[28]
       among any of these or them
dona eis requiem.
      (He would lose, not any one
              from among them.
Of all those given him
      he would lose none.)

       By the uteral marks
that make the covering stone an artefact.
       By the penile ivory
and by the viatic meats.
       Dona ei requiem.
Who was he? Who?
Himself at the cave-mouth
       the last of the father-figures
to take the diriment stroke
       of the last gigantic leader of
thick-felled cave-fauna?
Whoever he was
      Dona ei requiem
sempiternam.
(He would not lose him
      . . . *non perdidi*
ex eis quemquam.)[29]

       * * *

Upon all fore-times.
       From before time

From The Anathemata

his perpetual light
                     shines upon them.
                   Upon all at once
upon each one
whom he invites, bids, us to recall
when we make the recalling of him
                     daily, at the Stone.
When the offerant
      our *servos*, so theirs whose life is changed
not taken away[30]
                   is directed to say
                        Memento etiam.
After which it is allowed him then to say
                       Nobis quoque.
That we too may be permitted some part with these like John is!
                   as is Felicity.[31]
                 Through the same Lord
that gave the naiad her habitat
                   which is his proto-sign.
How else from the weathered mantle-rock
and the dark humus spread
(where is exacted the night-labour
           where the essential and labouring worm
saps micro-workings all the dark day long[32]
                   for his creature of air)
should his barlies grow
           who said
I am your Bread?

II

MIDDLE-SEA AND LEAR-SEA

Twelve hundred years
                close on
since of the Seven grouped Shiners
                one doused her light.[1]
Since Troy fired
                since they dragged him
                    widdershins[2]
without the wall.
When they regarded him:
his beauties made squalid, his combed gilt
                a matted mop
his bruised feet thonged
                under his own wall.
Why did they regard him
the decorous leader, *neque decor* . . .[3]
volneraque illa gerens[4] . . . many of them
under his dear walls?[5]

What centuries less
      since the formative epochs, the sign-years in Saturn's *tellus*,[6] in the middle lands of it? For even for the men with the *groma*,[7] even for the men of rule, whose *religio* is rule
                  for the world-orderers
                  for the world-syndicate
even for us
      whose robbery is conterminous with empire[8]

From The Anathemata

there was a: Once there was . . .
and wonder-years
and wanderers tall tale to tell
>   anabasis
>   by sea, by land
>   fore-chosen site
>   decalogue, dodecalogue graven
>   tabernacled flame
>   palladia come down.

Him up to heaven
>   in chariot-fire.[9]
The heaven-appointed beast of grey
>   to nourish the lily-white pair.
Horsed Dioscuri
>   to make 'em shape
restoring at the smothered centre, adjuvant at the caving flank;
the watering of mounts last groomed at heaven's horse-lines, the
care of celestial arms, their working parts fouled in terrestrial
war, the scrubbing-off of front-area muck from unearthly
equipment at a pond, in the market-place
>   in broad day
>   as large as life
>   a thing seen of many
so they do say.[10]
>   (They can show you the piscene.)[11]

>   How long, since
on the couch of time
>   departed myth
left ravished fact
till Clio, the ageing mid-wife,[12] found her

II: Middle-Sea and Lear-Sea

nine calends gone
      huge in labour with the Roman people?
[O, him! she said,
      himself, m'lord
the square-pushing Strider,[13] him?
and how should I?
It was dark, a very stormy night—the projecting cheek-guards, the rigid nasal-piece—brazen he wore it and darked his visage; twin-crested, and his mantling horse-tail shadowed dark *murex* my fair Aryan shoulders. Not he—not his proofed thorax neither, nor had he gratitude to unlace the mired greaves of surly iron—the squat Georgie!

    B'the clod smell on him *that's* what he *was*—before he got his papers,[14] by the manners of him. Yet—Verticordia, prevent us continually! but *which* way should grace turn matriarch-hearts?[15] . . . and how his glory filled the whole place where we were together.
And, now that I recall it:
    he first, with his butt-iron, marked the intersection and squared a space—he took his own time on that—and signed me to stand by, then, with a beck of his elbow, turned m' ample front to constant Arcturus, himself aligned to the southward, minding his dressing like the foot-mob masher he was,—or a haruspex checking his holy stance,
                                      the terrible inaugurator!
and, at the intersected place he caused our sacred commerce to be. Why yes—west he took himself off, on the base-line he traced and named when he traced it: *decumanus*. West-turn from his *kardo* I saw him go, over his right *transversus*.[16] From to rear of him I discerned his marcher's lurch—I'd breath to see that.
West-star, hers and all!
    brighting the hooped turn of his scapular-plates enough to show his pelvic sway and the hunch on his robber's shoulders. Though he was of the Clarissimi his aquila over me was robbery.[17]

From The Anathemata

'T's a great robbery
              —is empire.]

Half a millennium or so
              since
              out went the Lucomos
since we became
            abasileutos.
A good year?
            But little more
(the Kalends are erased or never reckoned)
since those hidden years
when an armaments commission
            (Tuscan at that)
could and did
effectively proscribe us:
            plant
            operatives
            raw metal.
That takes you back
            and aback.
The Urbs without edged iron
            can you credit it?
            Nudge Clio
she's apt to be musing.
Slap her and make her extol
            all or nothing.

Five hundred and thirty-nine years since the first consular year and the beginnings of the less uncertain sequences and the more defined contours.
How long since first we began to contrive

II: Middle-Sea and Lear-Sea

     on the loose-grained tufas
quarried about the place;
      incise, spaced and clear
on the carried marbles
       impose on the emblems:
SENATUSPOPULUSQUE . . . ?
       for all the world-nurseries
to say: Roma knows great A.[18]
For the world-connoisseurs to cant their necks and to allow:
   Yes, great epigraphers, let's grant 'em one perfected
aesthetic—and, of course, there's the portrait-busts.

    One hundred and sixty-seven years
since Tiberius Gracchus
       wept for the waste-land
and the end of the beginnings
       . . . and where I had a vineyard
On a very fruitful hill fenced and watered
       the syndicate's agent
pays-off the ranch operatives
      (his bit from the Urbs
waits in the car).

But sixty-eight years, since
      in came the Principate
and the beginnings of the end and the waxing of the megalopolis
and the acute coarsening of the forms, the conscious revivals, the
eclectic grandeur
      . . . the grand years
since we began our
     Good Time Coming.
And already, on every commodity and on the souls of men, the
branded numerals: *sexcenti sexaginta sex*.[19]

From The Anathemata

One thousand two hundred years
              since the Dorian jarls
rolled up the map of Arcady and the transmontane storm-groups fractured the archaic pattern.
              Within the hoop
of the iron years
              the age is obscure—
and is the age dark?
            The makers of anathemata can, at a pinch, beat out utile spares for the mobile columns or amulets for the raiding captains and the captains themselves bring certain specifications and new god-fears.
The adaptations, the fusions
the transmogrifications
              but always
the inward continuities
              of the site
              of place.

            From the tomb of the strife-years the new-born shapes begin already to look uncommonly like the brats of mother Europa.
We begin already to discern our own.
Are the proto-forms already ours?
Is that the West-wind on our cheek-bones?

But it's early—very grey and early in our morning and most irradiance is yet reflected from far-side Our Sea, the Nile moon still shines on the Hittite creatures and Crete still shows the Argives how.

II: Middle-Sea and Lear-Sea

Six centuries
                and the second Spring
and a new wonder under heaven:
                man-limb stirs
                      in the god-stones
and the kouroi
                are gay and stepping it
but stanced solemn.
And now is given a new stone indeed:
                the Good Calf-herd
for Rhonbos his *pastor bonus*
lifted up and adored
(and may we say of his moschophoros:
this pastoral Lord *regit me*?)[20]
                and the Delectable Korê:
by the radial flutes for her chiton, the lineal, chiselled hair
the contained rhythm of her
                is she Elenê Argive
or is she transalpine Eleanore
or our Gwenhwyfar[21]
                the Selenê of Thulê
                West-Helen?
She's all that and more
all korai, all parthenai made stone.[22]

Agelastos Petra . . . [23]
                and yet you smile from your stone.

                Not again, not now again
till on west-portals
in Gallia Lugdunensis
                when the Faustian lent[24] is come
and West-wood springs new
                (and Christ the thrust of it!)
and loud sings West-cuckoo
                (Polymnia, how shrill!)

From The Anathemata

      will you see her like
           if then.
Not again
      till the *splendor formarum*[25]
      when, under West-light
           the Word is made stone.
And when
      where, how or ever again?
                . . . or again?
Not ever again?
      never?
After the conflagrations
      in the times of forgetting?
in the loops between?
before the prides
      and after the happy falls?

Spes!
      answer me!!
How right you are—
      blindfold's best!
      But, where d'you think the flukes of y'r hook'll hold next—from the *feel* of things?

Down we come
      quick, but far
to the splendours
      to the skill-years
and the signed and fine grandeurs.
O yes, technique—but much more:
the god still is balanced
           in the man-stones

II: Middle-Sea and Lear-Sea

  but it's a nice thing
as near a thing as ever you saw.

One hundred and seventeen olympiads
since he contrived her:
    chryselephantine
    of good counsel
    within
      her Maiden's chamber
    tower of ivory
      in the gilded *cella*
    herself a house of gold.
Her grandeurs
  enough and to snare:
    West-academic
    West-hearts.
And her that he cast of Marathon-salvage
    of bronze
    erect
    without
    Promachos
    of the polis
    of Ouranos
Virgo Potens
  her alerted armament
land-mark for sea-course
Polias, and star of it
  but Tritogenian.
As a sea-mark then
  for the navigating officers.

Not always: *blue* Aegean
    nor smiling middle-*mare*.
The loomings and the dippings
    unsighted

From The Anathemata

what jack she wore
    unrecognized.
Who are you pray?[26]
    unanswered.
(Low, raked, Pelasgian Long Serpent
    for the low sea-mist.)
The shifts of wind
    the intermittent rain
      but Sunium
rounded.
Thirty-seven forty-five north
twenty-three thirty-nine east:
right ahead, beyond tanged Salamis, obscured Eleusis—
to port, Cleruchy island.[27]

And now his celestial influence gains:
      across the atmosphere
      on the water-sphere
and the wide sinus changes humour and the sea-hues
suffer change
      from Peloponnese Cenchréae
to the homing Attic deck-boy's
own Phaléron.
And suddenly:
    the build of us
      patterns dark the blueing waters
and shadow-gulls
perch the shadows of the yards across the starboard bow-wave
and on the quiet beam water.
          For his chariot
has crossed our course and he stands over Argolis, southward
and westing and darts back his tangent ray.

         What bells is that
when the overcast clears on a Mars' Venus-Day
Selene waxed, the sun in the Ram?[28]

II: Middle-Sea and Lear-Sea

Then's when the numbed and scurvied
                       top-tree boy
grins, like the kouroi[29]
from the straining top-stays:
Up she looms!
               three points on the starboard bow.
There's where her spear-flukes
                       pharos for you
day-star for the sea.
            The caulked old triton of us
            the master of us
he grins too:
            pickled, old, pelagios.
And was it the Lord Poseidon got him
               on the Lady of Tyre
queen of the sea-marts
                   or was his dam in far Colchis abed?
did an Argo's Grogram sire him?
       Certain he's part of the olden timbers: watch out for the
run o' the grain on him—look how his ancient knars are salted
and the wounds of the bitter sea on him.
               He's drained it again.
and again they brim it.
Is it the Iacchos
               in his duffle jacket
Ischyros with his sea-boots on?

There's those avers he's wintered with Cronos
under Arctophylax
             out of our *mare*
                   into their *See*.[30]

From The Anathemata

Was it dropped to half gale or did he get it bellyful from off-
shore
                    at hurricano strength
cataracted, sulphurous and all
                    when he stood into
Leir's river?
                    —they say he made Thulê.
Did he hold his course
                  mid-sleeve
where, at the wide gusset
                  it's thirty-five leagues?[31]
where Môr Iwerddon[32] meets
                  Mare Gallicum
where the seas of the islands war with the ocean, to white the
      horse-king's *insulae*
to blanch
              main and Ushant.[33]
Did Albion put down his screen of brume at:
   forty-nine fifty-seven thirty-four north five twelve four west[34]
to white-out the sea-margin east of northwards to confluent Fal,
and west over Mark's main towards where Trystan's sands run
out to land's last end?
Is that why
   from about forty-nine forty north five twenty west
      to forty-nine fifty-seven north four-forty west
he sighted no land
   till he first sighted it
a point before the beam in a north-westerly direction
about six leagues
            (by whatever card he knew)
and did he call it
            the Deadman?[35]
Then was when the trestle-tree boy
            from his *thalassa*
across the *mare*, between the Pillars
over the ocean . . .

II: Middle-Sea and Lear-Sea

        a weary time a weary time—
north-way is *Abendsee*—
            breasting the gulled grey, westing
over wave, wind's daughter
over billow, son of wave.
            Lying to, or going free
before a soldier's wind
            southers nording him
sou'westerlies nor'easting him
            or the blow backs
and easters west him off.
Now (true to a touched stone?)
            north, with the happy veer
and by good management.
Now north by east
            over the nine white grinders
            riding the daughters of the quern of islands[36]
kouroi from over *yr eigion*[37]
            making Dylan's *môroedd*[38]
            holding on towards
Igraine's *dylanau*[39]
            the eyes of her
towards the waters
            of the son of Amblet's daughter.[40]
What belles she can foam
            'twixt Uxantis and the Horn![41]
            And did Morgana's fay-light
abb the warp of mist
            that diaphanes the creeping ebb, or worse
                  the rapid flow
off Scylla's cisted West-site
            screening her felspar'd war
with the skerry-mill?[42]
Her menhirs
        DIS MANIBUS of
        many a *Schiller's* people

From The Anathemata

        many men
        of many a Clowdisley's ship's company:
for she takes nine
        in ten!
        But what Caliban's Lamia
rung him for his Hand of Glory![43]
(And where the wolf in the quartz'd height
        —O long long long
before the sea-mark light!—[44]
saliva'd the spume
        over Mark's lost hundred.
Back over
        the drowned tillage of Leonnoys
        over the smothered defences
over the hundred and forty *mensae* drowned
in the un-apsed *eglwysau*,[45] under.
Back to the crag-mound
        in the drowned *coed*
        under.)[46]

Now nor'-east by north
        now east by north, easting.
Sou' sou'-west the weather quarter
        by what slant of wind
they brought her into the Narrow Sea
        Prydain's *camlas*![47]
that they'll call Mare Austrum[48]
        Our thalassa!
The lead telling fifty in the chops.

Then was when the top-tree boy
from *his* thalassa over their *mare* . . .
        cried to his towny
before the mast-tree
        cries louder

II: Middle-Sea and Lear-Sea

(for across the weather)
                    to the man at the steer-tree:
Pretáni-shore!⁴⁹ Cassitérides!
                    we've rounded their Golden *Cornu*.⁵⁰
Mess-mates of mine
                    we shall be rich men
you shall have y'r warm-dugged Themis
and you, white Phoebe's lune
            . . . and laughless little Telphousa
what shipman's boy could ask another?
said she'd smile
                    for tin!
What ship's boy would lose her?
                    the skerry-mill rather!
rather the granite molars of the sea-Lamia.

                            But Albion's brume
begins to thin away, they've made a landfall yet they sight no
Ictian bay and must go a compass.

West now her head
                    she stands scarce six points
off the wind
                    and will that veer?
but no!
                    the smiler draws more south
to rejoice them.
And further souths, till east of south
                    as if the Maiden herself
were adjuvant.
                    But as that backs
that strengthens . . .
                    and for the dissipated brume
the squall-mist and the rain.

[163]

From **The Anathemata**

Close-cowled, in his mast-head stall the solitary cantor
cups his numbed hand to say his versicle:
                        Lánd afóre the beám to stárb'd
one to tẃo leagues.
And, as the ritual is, the respond is:
                        Lánd before the beám to stárboard
one to tẃo leagues.
                      But, from the drenched focsle
the stifled murmur is what each heart's wry gloss reads:
                      Rock ahead an' shoal to lee
less nor half a Goidel's league!
Is it then
                      each brined throat chanties?
We've made from Ilissus
                all the way
matlos of the Maiden
                all the way
                all the way
from Phaléron in the bay
matlos of the Maiden
                all the way b' star and day
                across the *mare*
                over the *See*[51]
to go to Dis in Lear's sea
                matlos of the Maiden
all for thalassócracy
all for thalassócracy
                Maiden help y'r own.

Wot'ld you do with the bleedin' owners?
Wot'ld you do with the bleedin' owners?
                What would you do with 'em?
put 'em in the long boat
put 'em in the long boat
                put them in the wrong boat

II: Middle-Sea and Lear-Sea

and let them sail her
>> over the seas to Dis.

Maiden help y'r own
Maiden help y'r own
>> Maiden aid us.

Themis, pray.
Phoebe, Telphousa[52]
>> pray.

Agelastos Petra
>> cleft for us!

Paphia remember us that are indentured to your mother.
And us marines, remember us
>> as belong to y'r panzer'd lover.

Sea-wives of Laconia
>> bid your Cytheréa

be mindful of her nativity.[53]
Ladies of Tyre and the Phoenician littoral pray The Lady to have a native pity on this ship's company—consider: how many inboard, along of us, belong to *her*!
In all the sun-lands of our cradle-sea
you many that are tutelar
>> regard our anathemata.

Pay our vows Iberian ladies
>> to the Lady of Iberia

for making by her coasts toward this place
we *did call* her by her name:
>> remind her.

In the parts of Liguria about Massilia and at Corbilo-on-Liger, our last port of call, implore the Three Mothers to recall what we have donated to all Gallia: almost all, letters most of all; nor least the love of our Ionian Artemis.
>> Phocaean Huntress, pray for us,

your sea-dogs hunted of the hungry sea.[54]
Vestals of Latium
>> if not yet taught of the Fisherman

From The Anathemata

give us your suffrage
                      whose lode is the Sea Star.

You that shall spread your hands over the things offered
make *memento* of us
and where the gloss reads *jungit manus*[55] count us among his argonauts whose argosy you plead,[56] under the sign of the things you offer.

                      Extend your hands
all you *orantes*
                      for the iron-dark shore
is to our lee
over the lead-dark sea
and schisted Ocrinum looms in fairish visibility
and white-plumed riders shoreward go
                      and
THE BIRDS DECLARE IT
                      that wing white and low
that also leeward go
                      go leeward to the tor-lands
where the tin-veins maculate the fire-rocks.
The birds
            have a home
in those rocks.

                      Her loosed hair for dog-vane, marking the grain of the gale, awaiting with confidence her gale-gift, Lamia waits at her sea-gate, within her land-lair.
Yet his scarfed stem
                  furrows the hull's lair
the knee of the head of her
ploughing the grinders

II: Middle-Sea and Lear-Sea

       white the wash
up over her flare to where her straked sides tumble home.
      Over her top-strake
green heads inboard rinse her floors to brine her up to her risings.[57]
O how he cons her!
    the old Pelasgian!
It might be Manannan himself, or the helmsman with the other *claves*, the gladiatorial vicar of seas.[58]
He yet holds on
    he's weathered Ocrinum
      already he stands on
toward Bolerion.[59]
Drove of world-wind, sun's obedient daughter
      hove down of wind, wave's mother
        pooped of billow, son of wave.
Now he stands her in for the isthmus
bearing nor' nor' west three-quarter west.
Shipping a sea
     yet he rounds her to
now are the eyes of her
      due toward her destined haven
      due over the bow-wash
a sky-shaft brights the whited mole
wind-hauled the grinders
      white the darked bay's wide bowl
white echeloned daughters of the island mill
deploy from twenty-fathom water to the inner shoal
spume-blind into the skerry-mill
     he bears on his port of call
distant three leagues and a quarter.

Did he berth her?
    and to schedule?
by the hoar rock in the drowned wood?[60]

From VII

MABINOG'S LITURGY

                Brow of Helen!
hide your spot that draws the West.
No! nor cast eyes here of green or devastating grey
                    are any good at all.
Had she been on Ida mountains
to whose lap would have fallen y'r golden ball, if not to hers that laps the unicorn?[1]
                                And you!
She has your hunter's moon as well.
Vanabride! y'r cats come to her call.[2]
Whose but hers, the Lady of Heaven's hen?[3] and, as Dürer knew, the butterfly is proper to her himation.[4]

Look to y'r title, Day-star o' the Harbour![5]
                    . . . in all her parts
tota pulchra
more lovely than our own Gwenhwyfar[6]
                       when to the men of this Island
she looked at her best[7]
                    at mid-night
three nights after the solstice-night, the sun in the Goat, in the second moon after Calangaeaf;[8] with the carried lights that are ordinary to her before her and the many *plygain*-lights[9] special to this night about her; the *yntred*[10] sung, the synaxis done, at the beginning of The Offering proper,[11] when they light the offertory-light that burns solitary on the epistle side; standing within the screen (for she was the wife of the Bear of the

From VII: Mabinog's Liturgy

Island)[12] and toward the lighted board; in cloth of Grass of Troy and spun Iberian asbestos,[13] and under these ornate wefts the fine-abb'd Eblana flax, maid-worked (as bleached as will be her cere-cloth of thirty-fold when they shall intone for her . . . *pro anima famulae tuae*[14]) and under again the defeasible and defected image of him who alone imagined and ornated us, made fast of flesh her favours, braced bright, sternal and vertibral, to the graced bones bound.

                                                   If her gilt, unbound
(for she was consort of a *regulus*) and falling to below her sacral bone, was pale as standing North-Humber barley-corn, here, held back in the lunula of Doleucothi[15] gold, it was paler than under-stalks of barley, held in the sickle's lunula. So that the pale gilt where it was by nature palest, together with the pale river-gold where it most received the pallid candle-sheen, rimmed the crescent whiteness where it was whitest.

        Or, was there already silver to the gilt?
For if the judgmatic smokes of autumn seemed remote, John's Fires were lit and dead, and, as for gathering knots of may—why not talk of maidenheads?
Within this arc, as near, as far off, as singular, as the whitest of the Seven Wanderers, of exorbitant smoothness, yet puckered a little, because of the extreme altitude of her station, for she was the spouse of the Director of Toil,[16] and, because of the toil within,

                          her temples gleamed
among the carried lights hard-contoured as Luna's rim, when in our latitudes in winter time, she at her third phase, casts her shadow so short that the out-patrol moves with confidence, so near the zenith she journeys.[17]

                                      If as Selenê in highness
so in influence, then as Helenê too:[18] by her lunations the neapings and floodings, because of her the stress and drag.

        . . . for she was the king our uncle's wedlocked wife and he our father and we his sister's son.[19]

From The Anathemata

And from where over-gown and under-gown and *linea* draped the clavicled torus of it, her neck-shaft of full entasis, as though of Parian that never ages, still as a megalith, and as numinous:
                        yet, as limber to turn
as the poised neck at the forest-fence
                    between find and view
too quick, even for the eyes of the gillies of Arthur, but seen of the forest-ancraman (he had but one eye)
                        between decade and *Gloria*.

                    Downward from this terminal, down from the wide shoulders (for she was a daughter of the *tyrannoi* of Britain and these Arya were *cawraidd*)[20] down over the high-laced buskins (these the *Notitia*[21] permitted) to where the supple Andalusian buck-skin, freighted from Córdoba, cased her insteps (for all the transmarine negotiators, prospectors, promoters, company-floaters and *mercatores* laded and carried for her) covering all but the lower eyelet-rings and the thong-tags and other furnishings of polar ivory
                    to obtain which
who but Manawydan himself, on the whale-path, but four and half degrees of latitude without the arctic parallel, two hundred and twenty nautical miles south-east by south of Islont[22] with Thor's Fairy-Haven[23] Isles looming on his starboard beam about six Gaulish leagues, alone and by himself—except for his *môr-forwyn*-mates[24]—running free with the wind on the starboard side, carried away and handsomely, the rare dexter tooth of the living bull narwhal that bluff-nosed the southwester nose-ender with spiralled ivories lancing the bright spume scud.
                      The cruising old *wicing*!
This he averred he achieved on his ocean-trip to the Thing-Ness in Gynt-land,[25] his *hiraeth*[26] upon him, some fifteen days out from his *dinas* in Cemeis in Demetia[27]

From VII: Mabinog's Liturgy

        (where he latins his oghams).
Plotting his course by the North Drift route that streams him warm to Hordaland
        to Noroway o'er his faem
over the gurly brim in his mere-hengest
        (he's stepped the Yggdrasil for mast!)
To the Horder's moot in Norvegia
        over the darkening mere-flood
on a Gwener-Frigdaeg noon.[28]
        (To add a bit *more*
to his old *mabinogion*?[29]
        Will he Latin that *too*
to get some Passion into his Infancy?
        By the Mabon!! he will
when he runes the Croglith,[30]
        in all the white bangors[31]
of the islands of the sea
        where there is salt
on the Stone within the *pared*.)[32]

Or, was he a liar?
        Did he and his back-room team contrive this gleaming spoil from fungus by Virgil's arts in Merlin's Maridunum?[33] Or, did he barter 'em, ready-made-up, in Bristol? He might have done either, the old conjurer!

        Downward then obscuring all, over all the numinous whole, over all the knit parts other than the column of her neck and the span-broad forehead and whatever strong enchantment lay between forehead and chin:
        We are not concerned with portrait but it can be inferred that of her eyes, one was blemish'd.

Over other than all this, and excepting only these terminal forms, mantling the whole leaning column (which was the live base for

From The Anathemata

these) covering for the most part the handsome, well-shaped Dalmatian tunic of gold stuff inter-threaded green (the stitched-on dark laticlaves kermes-dipt) that had beneath it the convenient, well-fitting, glossy under-gown of shining fire-stone, that hid all but entirely the long, bleached, well-adjusted, comfortable vest that sheathed immediately the breathing marble.[34]
                      Habiting all and over all
from top to toe (almost)
ample and enfolding
                      in many various folds
with the many lights
                      playing variously on the folds
her wide *lacerna*.[35]
                    (As near the sacred *murex* a length o' cloth as ever come out of a Silchester madder-vat!)
                    And moreover patterned the colour of gorse-buds in forms as *apis*-like as may be.
(Ischyros and all his Basils! what will they say of that at Caer Gustennin?)[36]
                    Edged and lined throughout
with dappled vairs of marten and pale kinds of wild-cat:
                    It's cold in West-chancels.
So, wholly super-pellissed of British wild-woods, the chryselephantine column (native the warm blood in the blue veins that vein the hidden marbles, the lifted abacus of native gold) leaned, and toward the Stone.

                    And on and over the stone the spread board-cloths and on this three-fold linen the central rectangle of finest linen and on the spread-out part of this linen the up-standing calix that the drawn-over laundered folds drape white.[37]
                    And before the palled cup
the open dish and on the shallow dish and in the wide bowl of the stemmed cup

From VII: Mabinog's Liturgy

>>the three waiting *munera*:

Of Ceres

>from the reserve-*granaria*

>>(for Elbe-men blacken with red fire the east wheat-belt, and nothing through from Loidis,[38] and elsewhere the situation is obscure and Nials gathering hostages[39] gather also the white sign, and then on top of all and everywhere the blackening by grey rain for three successive years of rotten harvest).

Of Liber

>perhaps from over the Sleeve

made confluent with the lucid gift
our naiads never fail to bring

>>parthenogenic from the rock

quick by high valleys, or

>meandering slow and

by the wide, loamed ways, by sallowed way

>sign the whole anatomy of Britain

with his valid sign

>(out of where the nereids

bring in the shoal-gift: also Him, in sign).
No wonder

>the proud column
>>leaned

to such a board
even before the Magian handling and the Apollinian word[40] that shall make of the waiting creatures, in the vessels on the board-cloths over the Stone, his body who said, DO THIS

>for my Anamnesis.[41]
>By whom also this column was.

He whose fore-type said, in the Two Lands

>>I AM BARLEY.[42]

It was fortunate for the innate *boneddigion*[43] of Britain that when at the prayer *Qui pridie*[44] she was bound as they to raise her face, she as they, faced the one way, or else when the lifted Signa

From The Anathemata

shone they had mistaken the object of their Latria; to add to the taint of the Diocese of Britain an impulse more eccentric from the New Mandate than is the innate bias of the heresiarchs of Britain.

NOTES TO *THE ANATHEMATA*

Preface

1. The actual words are *coacervavi omne quod inveni*, and occur in *Prologue II* to the *Historia*.

2. Quoted from the translation of *Prologue I*. See *The Works of Gildas and Nennius*, J. A. Giles, London, 1841.

3. See Gogarty, *As I was Going Down Sackville Street*, p. 287. London, 1937.

4. Blodeuedd, blod-ei-eth, ei as in height, eth as in nether, accent on middle syllable; from *blodau* flowers. The name given in Welsh mythology to the woman made by magical processes from various blossoms.

5. Or whatever the translation might be. Anwyl's dictionary gives: lord, king, ruler, sovereign, prince. But none of these are satisfactory. The word is connected with *gwlad*, country or land and in modern Welsh *gwledig*, used as an adjective, implies something rural or rustic. As a noun it belongs only to the early Dark Ages; when it was used only of very important territorial rulers; it was used of Maximus the emperor, it was used by Taliessin, of God. Significantly it was never used of Arthur, because he was a leader of a mobile cavalry force, and not a territorial ruler.

6. See commentary by C. S. Lewis, 'Williams and the Arthuriad', in *Arthurian Torso*, 1948.

7. Who wrote a poetry that was counter-Renaissant, creaturely yet otherworld-ordered, ecstatical yet technically severe and ingenious, concerned with conditions of the psyche, but its images very much of the soma; metaphysical, but not un-intrigued by the physics of the period; English, but well represented by names hardly English; thus still posing interesting questions for those specialists whose business it is to research into that epoch. A research which continues. We wish them good hunting.

From The Anathemata

8. A book from which I have already quoted, by Thomas Gilby, O.P.
 The distinction compactly put by Fr Gilby in this passage has indeed been expressed and many of its implications dwelt upon by my friend the late Mr Eric Gill; and I should like to take this opportunity of acknowledging my indebtedness to those fruitful conversations with Mr Gill in years gone by, regarding this business of man-the-artist. For he possessed, in conversation, a Socratic quality, which, even in disagreement, tended to clarification.

9. Or did so forty or fifty years back.

10. The actual form now in use is: '. . . *benedictam, adscriptam, ratam, rationabilem, acceptabilemque facere digneris*' and is part of the oblational prayers in the Roman mass. As it stands in its Latin form it is only of the fourth century. It is, however, said by liturgical scholars to link with forms in use in the Greek-speaking Roman church about the beginning of the third century; a date as near to St John or to 'Boadicea' as are you and I to William Blake or Maréchal Ney.

11. I seem to recall a passage in *The Shape of the Liturgy* (Dix) where the author, referring to the words 'these thy creatures of bread and wine' in the *Book of Common Prayer*, rightly says (as far as I can remember) that these words suggest that bread and wine are simply fruits of the earth, whereas this is not strictly so. At all events that is the distinction which I wish to emphasize here. It is one which I think has very important implications and corollaries.

12. See note 41 to page 173 of text with regard to 'recalling' in this connection.

13. Unless of course we regarded that religion as being *exclusively* concerned with an attitude of mind or state of soul.

14. Except in some few denominations, e.g. the Society of Friends. Not that these escape either; for they employ forms of some kind and a genuine and very decent procedure. And where there is order and sensitivity to the conserving of a form, there is the muse.

15. I use the word *disciplinae* here because I can't think of an English word which covers what I intend: the various modes and traditions of doing this or that, from bowling a hoop to engraving on copper; from 'Kiss in the Ring' to serving at Mass; from forming fours (or threes) to Rolle of Hampole's *Form of Perfect Living*; from Rugby Union Rules to the rules that governed court etiquette in the Welsh medieval codes; from the mixing of water-colours to the mixing of pig-food; from mending the fire to mending the fire-step; from the making of blackbird pie to the

Notes

making of a king; from the immemorial nursery methods of reminding children that they are not laws to themselves to the three extinguishings of the lighted flax that at his coronation remind the Pontiff Maximus of much the same truth, together with the words, which at each extinguishing they say to him: *Sancte Pater, sic transit gloria mundi*. For in a sense all *disciplinae* are warnings 'This is the way to make the thing, that way won't do at all'.

16. I prefer 'myth' to 'mythus', but owing to such sentences as 'She said she'd got some fags, but it was a pure myth' the meaning of 'myth' is liable to misunderstanding even in the most serious connections.

    Unfortunately *The Shorter Oxford English Dictionary* (1933) defines 'myth' as 'A purely fictitious narrative, etc.' Yet we sing in the Liturgy '*Teste David cum Sibylla*' and clearly the Sibyl belongs to what, for the Christian Church, is an extra-revelational body of tradition. But such bodies of tradition are not to be described as 'purely fictitious', yet they are certainly properly described as 'myth'. I choose this example from among innumerable others, because of the accepted rule that the public prayer of an institution is a sure gauge to the mind of the institution that employs that prayer. I don't mind the rather academic 'mythus' but I don't see why we should have the English form 'myth' permanently separated from its primal innocence, from the Greek *mythos*, which, I understand, means a word uttered, something told. Then we should rightly speak of the myth of the Evangel, a myth devoid of the fictitious, an utterance of the Word, a 'pure myth'.

Rite and Fore-time

1. See the Roman Mass, the Prayer of Consecration, beginning 'Which oblation do thou . . . ascribe to, ratify, make reasonable. . . .'

2. Cf. the same, '. . . in sanctas ac venerabiles manus suas. . . .'

3. Cf. the derivation of the word chancel, from *cancelli*, lattice bars.

4. King Pellam in Malory's *Morte d'Arthur* is lord of the Waste Lands and the lord of the Two Lands.

5. Cf. 'Every scribe instructed in the kingdom of heaven is like to a man who is a householder, who bringeth forth out of his treasure new things and old.' See the Common of a Virgin Martyr, Mass 2, Gospel.

6. Cf. Middle-English poem: *Of a rose a lovly rose* 'Every day it schewit in prystes hond'.

7. *Mola salsa*, the cake of spelt and salt made by the Roman Vestals and used

From The Anathemata

at the purification of sacrifices; and cf. Mark IX, 49–50, which indicates the same use of salt in Jewish rites.

8. 'tumulus' because the tumuli, the barrows on our downlands and hill-sites, were essentially burial places and because a Christian altar, by the requirements of Canon Law, and in observance of a use at least as old as the fourth century, should contain relics of the dead. Cf. at the beginning of Mass the priest kisses the altar, saying, '. . . by the merits of thy saints whose relics are here . . .' and cf. the Offertory prayer *Suscipe sancta trinitas* in which the words occur 'and of these here' (*et istorum*). This prayer is very explicit; it says that the oblation is offered to the Trinity, in remembrance of the Passion, Resurrection and Ascension and in honour of the Theotokos, of certain named saints and those whose relics lie under the particular altar at which the Mass is being celebrated, together with all the saints departed.

9. See *Le Morte d'Arthur*, xvii, 20, 'Everyman' edition; modernized spelling: 'the holy dish wherein I ate the lamb on Sher-Thursday'.

The textual authority on Malory's works, Professor Vinaver, gives 'on Estir Day' for Caxton's 'on sherthursdaye' and notes the latter as a corrupt variant. A French source is given as *le jour de Pasques*.

But as the words 'Thursday' and 'the holy dish' are, by gospel, rite, calendar and cultus, indissolubly connected, I regard Caxton's variant as most fortunate. Hence the use of 'sherthursdaye' here and in the title of Section 8 of this book.

10. The conditions determining the exact time of the Passover were that the moon must be at the full, the vernal equinox past and the sun in Aries. The fixed date of the feast was the fourteenth day of the first month, Nisan; and if that date was due to fall before these conjunctions the necessary number of days were inserted into the calendar in order to postpone it. Subsidiary causes influencing this intercalation, such as the backwardness of the crops and the beasts, are also mentioned in the rabbinical writings. There was as yet no fixed calendar and adjustments were made each year on an empirical basis.

See Schürer, *Hist. of Jewish People*, Div. 1, Vol. II, Appendix. 'The Jewish and Macedonian months compared with the Julian calendar.' (Eng. Trans. Edtn. 1890.)

11. Cf. the instructions given to Peter and John in the Passion according to Luke.

'As you go into the city there shall meet you a man carrying a pitcher of water: follow him into the house where he entereth in . . . And he will show you a large dining-room furnished: and there prepare.' (Trans. of Vulgate.)

Notes

The passage also partly reflects memories I have of walking in the lanes of Jerusalem, the excessive dryness and white dust, the low arched entries and stairs up into cool interior rooms.

12. Cf. song, *Green grow the rashes O*
    'Four for the Gospel makers'.
    Of the four evangelists, Matthew was present at the supper. John, one of the two 'Sons of Thunder', was also present. Whether this was the author of the Fourth Gospel has been much debated. Here the traditional identification is taken for granted.

13. 'the right-board'—starboard.

14. Kerioth, a village of Judea from which Judas came, hence 'the Iscariot'.

15. The great rock over which the temple of Jerusalem was built was regarded not only as the navel of the world but as separating the waters of the abyss under the earth from the celestial waters.

16. It is usually supposed that Abraham moved north-west up the Euphrates valley from 'Ur of the Chaldees' about 2,000 BC. The cultivation of grain had begun in Mesopotamia at least by 4,000 BC.

17. The first examples of visual art so far (1940) discovered date from about 20,000 BC. There is evidence of artefacture, of a sort, twenty thousand and more years earlier still, e.g. flints and marked stones, but these are hardly 'visual art' in the accepted sense.

18. In Northern myth, Uhland is the abode of the gods of the atmosphere, the *Luftraum*. Vanabride is Freyja, a kind of Teutonic Venus. White cats draw her car across the blue sky and her myth seems in part confused with that of Frigg the wife of Odin. She is the most beautiful of the Vanir and half the departed (who die bravely) are hers.

19. The reference is to the Benedictine abbey of Melk, in Austria, which I am told was one of the great centres of church music.

20. Cf. the *Limes Raetiae*, which marked the limits of the civilized world in the Danube district.

21. The reference is to the first work of plastic art in-the-round known to us, the little limestone sculpture just over four inches high, of very ample proportions, known as 'the Venus of Willendorf'. It is dated, I believe, as contemporary with some of the recently discovered Lascaux cave-paintings, and is of the same Aurignacian culture of 20–25,000 BC. If it is a 'Venus' it is very much a Venus Genetrix, for it emphasizes in a very emphatic manner the nutritive and generative physiognomy. It is rather the earliest example of a long sequence of mother-figures,

From The Anathemata

earth-mothers and mother goddesses, that fuse in the Great-Mother of settled civilizations—not yet, by a long, long way, the Queen of Heaven, yet, nevertheless, with some of her attributes; in that it images the generative and the fruitful and the sustaining, at however primitive and elementary, or, if you will, 'animal' a level; though it is slovenly to use the word 'animal' of any art-form, for the making of such forms belongs only to man.

22. *O vere beata nox*, 'O truly blessed night'. See the *Exsultet* chanted by the deacon at the blessing of the Paschal Candle which is lighted from a fire of charcoal newly kindled by striking flint. This occurs once in the annual cycle, in the spring, on Easter Saturday. From the new fire so kindled the lamps and candles used during the ensuing twelve months are subsequently lit.

23. Although Neanderthal man of 40 to 60,000 BC appears not to be regarded by the anthropologists as a direct ancestor of ourselves, nevertheless it would seem to me that he must have been 'man', for his burial-sites show a religious care for the dead. At his places of interment the covering stones have revealed ritual markings; moreover food-offerings, weapons and possibly a life-symbol (a horn) have been found buried with him. Further, the hollow markings ('cup-marks') are similar to those which characterize the sacred stones of tens of thousands of years afterwards, in the New Stone Age culture which began, as far as Western Europe is concerned, as recently as *c.* 5,000 BC, or later, to continue among some primitive peoples to this day, in some parts of the world.

24. The Mirriam are a people of the Shendam Division of the Plateau Province of Nigeria. The men of this tribe are not totally naked, but the women in general are, except for ornaments of bamboo pith. [. . .]

25. Cf. the term Hebdomadarius, which is used of that member of a chapter or religious community whose office it is to lead in choir. His or her duties last a week.

26. The first cupolas or rounded vaults in Europe were made by men of the Megalithic culture in Southern Spain, in the first and second millennium BC. We are, in our text, referring to conditions in the twentieth millennium BC or earlier.

27. 'It was no doubt in the . . . Tertiary Age . . . that the earliest forms of man first came into existence' . . . 'Thus it was probably only after the expulsion of man from the Paradise of the Tertiary World . . . that he made those great primitive discoveries of the use of clothing, of

weapons and above all of fire, which rendered him independent of the changes of climate. . . .' Dawson, *Age of the Gods*, 1929.

28. See '. . . *opera enim illorum sequuntur illos*' in the Epistle for the Third Mass of All Souls' Day. *Apocalypse* xiv, 13. These *opera* are of course those that follow supernatural faith whereby the doers gain supernatural benefit. But I suppose it is permitted to use the same words analogously of those *opera* which we call artefacts, which man alone can cause to be.

    The dictionary defines artefact as an artificial product, thus including the beaver's dam and the wren's nest. But I here confine my use of the word to those artefacts in which there is an element of the extra-utile and the gratuitous. If there is any evidence of this kind of artefacture then the artefacturer or artifex should be regarded as participating *directly* in the benefits of the Passion, because the extra-utile is *the* mark of man.

    For which reason the description 'utility goods' if taken literally could refer only to the products of sub-man.

29. Quoted from the Good Friday Liturgy. '. . . I have not lost of them any single one.'

30. See the preface in the Mass for All Souls' Day and for all Masses of the departed '. . . Tuis enim fidelibus, Domine, vita mutatur non tollitur.' 'For thy faithful, O Lord, life is changed not taken away.'

31. The commemoration of the dead in the Latin rite follows the consecration and begins: 'Remember them, O Lord, thy servants'. This prayer for the departed is followed immediately by: 'To us also, sinners, grant some part . . . with John, etc., Felicity, etc., . . . into whose company admit us . . . through Christ our Lord'. The prayer concludes with a kind of recalling of the fruits of the land ('hallow, quicken and bless these and give them to us') without which no sacrament could be.

32. Darwin, in *The Formation of Vegetable Mould through the Action of Worms*, Ch. I, says in effect that worms do their 'day-labour light deny'd' in two senses, in that they work only by night and are blind, yet are far from being insensitive to light.

    General Note to Section I. The findings of the physical sciences are necessarily mutable and change with fresh evidence or with fresh interpretation of the same evidence. This is an important point to remember with regard to the whole of this section of my text where I employ ideas based on more or less current interpretations of archaeological and anthropological data. Such interpretations, of whatever degree of probability, remain hypothetical. The layman can but employ for his own purposes the pattern available during his lifetime.

From The Anathemata

The poet in *c.* 1200 could make good use of a current supposition that a hill in Palestine was the centre of the world. The poet of the seventeenth century could make use of the notion of gravitational pull. The abiding truth behind those two notions would now, in both cases (I am told), be differently expressed. But the poet, of whatever century, is concerned only with how he can use a current notion to express a permanent mythus.

Middle-Sea and Lear-Sea

1. At the fall of Troy one of the Pleiades is said to have been extinguished.

2. It is to be supposed that Achilles, in chasing, or in the other tradition, dragging, Hector around the defences of Troy, did so anti-sunwise; as it was to unbind the protection of the city and not to secure it. (See on this matter, Jackson Knight *Virgil's Troy*, p. 23, and *Cumaean Gates*, p. 90.)

3. See Isaias LIII, 2, '*non est species et neque decor*' (Vulgate), 'there is no beauty in him nor comeliness' (A.V.).

4. See 'Squalentem barbam et concretos sanguine crines
   Volneraque illa gerens quae circum plurima muros
   Accepit patrios.' *Aeneid II* 277–9.

5. See what is said above of Hector, 'His beard made squalid, his hair concreted with blood, bearing the many wounds he had received around the wall of his *patria*', and also 'O light of the whole Trojan world' and '*Heu mihi!* what was his aspect now, and how changed' and 'By what intolerable cause are your bright features made horrible to us' and other such phrases referring to the defilement of the beauty of the hero in *Aeneid II*. All this inevitably recalls 'he had no beauty that we should desire him . . . yet did we esteem stricken', etc., and other passages in the Prophets and also in the narrative of the Passion itself and in subsequent devotional writings, concerning the indignities suffered by the Redeemer, both within and without the walls of his *patria*.

6. Saturn's *tellus* = Italy.

7. The Roman surveyor's measuring instrument.

8. Cf. Augustine, *City of God*, IV, 4.

9. It will be recalled that the 'Twelve Tables' of Roman tradition were originally ten, that the temple of Vesta tabernacled the sacred fire, that the sacred shields came down from, that Romulus was assumed up to,

Notes

heaven; that Scriptural tradition offers certain near parallels. We Europeans have participated of both traditions—of the one by right of cultural and racial inheritance, of the other by 'adoption and grace'— *Teste David cum Sibylla.*

10. Cf. the traditions surrounding the battle of Lake Regillus which, very long before we had so much as heard of Livy, the majority of us learned by heart from *The Lays* and owing to the easy facility of Macaulay's rhymes are unable, if we would, to forget. From Macaulay we first sensed that we belonged to the Roman world and that Vesta, Juno, Romulus, Praeneste, 'reedy Thrasymene', and most of all 'the Great Asylum', had an evocative power over us.

11. I am told the fountain where Castor and Pollux washed their armour after the Battle of Lake Regillus is still shown to visitors in Rome.

12. *Kleio*, 'she that extols', the Muse of History.

13. Perhaps it has already become necessary to note that around about the period 1914–18 and subsequently, a 'square-pusher' was a soldier out courting. I do not know if the expression is still current among soldiers. See the surname of Mars, *Gradivus*.

14. Mars was an agriculturalist before he was a soldier.

15. Venus, under the title Verticordia, Turner of Hearts, was supplicated as the special guardian of fidelity and in this capacity was the patroness of matrons.

16. Cf. the sacred routine followed by the Roman surveyors in the laying out of sites: the north-south bearing was called *kardo* and the east-west was called *decumanus*, and the left and right limits of the square were each called *limes transversus*.

17. Cf. Song of Songs, II, 4, 'and his banner over me was love'. And cf. how those training for the Survey used the title Clarissimus.

18. I had in mind a child's rhyme which I can but hazily recall, but which I think ran somewhat as follows:
    'Tiddle taddle titmouse
    Flora* knows great A
    B and C and D and E
    G, H, I and J and K.'
    * Or Doris, or Augustus or whatever the name of the child reciting it.

19. Cf. The Apocalypse of St John, xiii, 16–18.

20. Cf. the superb early sixth-century-BC fragmentary marble figure of a man

From The Anathemata

carrying a calf dedicated by a person called Rhonbos on the Acropolis. One is inevitably reminded of the centuries later, immeasurably inferior, well-known Graeco-Roman figure called the 'Good Shepherd', adaptations of which are familiar to Christians. The smile on a kouros is Greek, the stance Egyptian.

Cf. also the opening words of the Vulgate Psalm 22, 'The Lord rules me', which is Ps 23 in the A.V., 'The Lord is my Shepherd'.

21. Gwenhwyfar, gwen-hooy-varr, stress accent on the middle syllable; Guenevere.

22. I was thinking in particular of the sixth-century-BC Athenian statuette of a young woman, known to connoisseurs as the 'Beautiful Kore', and of others of the archaic period which in some ways share a certain similarity of feeling with some carved queens of the twelfth-century-AD in the West—at Chartres for instance. Kore, maiden; korai, parthenai, maidens.

23. I am associating the rock called Agelastos Petra, 'the laughless rock', at pre-Hellenic Eleusis (where the modelled cult-object in its stone cist within the cleft of the rock, represented the female generative physiognomy) with the Megaron-type buildings on Troy-rock where Helen was the pearl-to-be-sought within the traversed and echeloned defences of the city. But apart from this association we can accurately describe the hall of Priam as 'laughless', and certainly Helen was a margaron of great price.

24. The reference is to Spengler's use of the term 'Faustian' which he employs to describe the Celto-Latin-Germanic-Western-Christian culture which by his theory had its springtime in the earliest middle ages. This is to say its freshest vitality was over before 1300.

25. Cf. the technical term *splendor formae* used of Beauty in Thomist philosophy. I borrow the terminology to use it analogously and in a non-philosophical, everyday sense and in the plural, of those visible 'forms' of art-works, which, after all, derive their outward 'splendour' from the *forma*, i.e. the unseen informing principle, referred to in the technical language of the definition.

26. See the formula used in questioning the identity of another ship fallen in with at sea.

27. The island of Aegina.

28. See note 10 to page 141 above and see in the account of the Passion according to the three synoptic writers 'darkness over all the earth until the ninth hour'.

Notes

29. Kouroi, as used of archaic Greek male statues; cf. p. 155 above.
30. Pronounce as in the German *die See* (zay) and so rhyming with *mare* above and Thulê below.
31. Cf. song *Spanish Ladies*, verse 2.
    'From Ushant to Scilly is thirty-five leagues.'
32. Môr Iwerddon, Irish Sea, mōrr ee-werr-thon, accent on third syllable.
33. The name of 'Mark', king of Cornwall in the Iseult story, is, in Welsh, *March* which means a stallion; the Scilly Isles were part of his domain.
    The action of the Atlantic tides meeting the waters of the English Channel is, I am told, strongly felt along the Breton mainland and around the Island of Ushant, just as it is on the Cornish side, or much more so.
34. The bearing of the Lizard Light.
35. See song *Spanish Ladies*, verse 3:
    'The first land we made, it is callèd the Deadman'.
    Another version reads:
    'The first land we sighted was callèd the Dodman'.
36. The Scandinavian sea-god Ægir ('sea') was surnamed 'the island mill' and his nine daughters are the waves that grind the rocks or skerries.
37. *Yr eigion*, the deep (from the Latin, *Oceanus*), pronounce urr ei-gion, accent on first syllable of *eigion*, 'g' hard, ei as in height.
38. *môroedd*, seas, mōrr-oithe.
39. *dylanau*, seas, dul-an-ei (as ei in height), accent on middle syllable. This common noun is derived from the proper noun Dylan (dul-an, accent on first syllable). Dylan was the son of the virgin Aranrhod; he took at his birth the nature of the waves.
40. The name of Arthur's mother in Romance literature is Igraine, the Welsh form is Eigr and *eigr* as a common noun means belle or maiden. She was one of the daughters of Anlawdd Wledig.
    Cf. the theory that relates Anlawdd Wledig with Abloyc son of Cunedda Wledig and in turn equates these names with Hamlet prince of Denmark through such forms as e.g. Amlodi, Amblethus, Hamblet. (See Israel Gollancz, *The Sources of Hamlet*.)
41. Uxantis is Ushant and the Horn is Cornwall. In Celtic as in Latin *cornu* meant horn, in modern Welsh *corn*. Hence the Old English compound *Cornwealas*, 'the Welsh of the horn'.

From The Anathemata

42. Cf. the stone cist discovered in a large barrow on one of the smaller islands of the Scillies, which whole group is remarkably rich in megalithic burial-sites. Scilly, as with the Classical Scylla and the common noun 'skerry', means a rock in the sea.

43. Cf. as typic of the innumerable losses off the Scillies the two most popularly remembered: In 1875 the *Schiller* whose 300 dead are buried on St Mary's; in 1707 the flagship and other vessels of the squadron of Sir Clowdisley Shovell together with 800 men in his ship and himself. Cf. the Scillonian saying that nine are dead by water for one dead in the course of nature.

   Cf. the report that Sir Clowdisley was washed alive to shore but was murdered by a Cornish woman for the jewels on his fingers. Lamia, a land vampire.

44. Cf. the Wolf Rock Light, between Mount's Bay and the Scillies.

45. Latin *mensae*, altars, rhymes with Welsh *eglwysau*, churches; eg-loois-ei, ei as in height, accent on second syllable.

   Cf. the identification of the Leonnoys or Lyonesse of Romance literature with the sea-area beyond Land's End; and the independent native Cornish tradition of the submergence of a countryside with the loss of one hundred and forty churches in that area.

46. Cf. the disputed theory that an old Cornish compound word meaning 'the hoar rock in the wood' is an authentic pre-inundation site-name for the rocky island now called St Michael's Mount.
   coed (koid) wood.

47. Prydain, Britain; prud-ein, ei as in height. *Camlas*, a channel; cam-lass, the 's' is very strongly sibilant, accent on first syllable.

48. At one period the English Channel was known as 'the South Sea' in Latin MS. See Ordnance Survey Map, *Britain in the Dark Ages*, South Sheet.

49. Pronounce pret-tan-ee, accent on middle syllable. The name by which the inhabitants of the British Isles were known to Antiquity before Caesar was the Priteni or the Pretani. Cf. Old Welsh, the *Priten*. It still survives in the Modern Welsh name for the island of Britain itself, Prydain.

50. The Horn allusion demanded my quite inaccurate 'rounded'.

51. Pronounced as in *die See*, rhyming with 'day' and '*mare*'.

52. These names of the three sweethearts of the matelots each connote various aspects of femaleness: the earth, the seasons, the fates, the sibylline art,

Notes

the menstrual cycle, the moon, so the tides, the huntress, the mother. Telphousa in particular has affinities with Delphi and so with Petra Agelastos. Cf. note 23 to page 155 above.

53. Both Paphos on Cyprus and the Island of Cythera off the Laconian coast were claimed as the place where Aphrodite was delivered from the womb of her mother, the sea. The nearness of Cyprus to the Syrian coast may indicate a route by which Es Sitt, The Lady (as they still call her among the Arabs of Palestine), came to Hellas and so to us.

54. Corbilo at the mouth of the Loire was one of the distribution ports of the tin-traders in pre- and early-historic times. It was from the Phocaean settlement at Marseilles that Ionian influences infiltrated Gaul, and Phocaean sea-men are known to have spread the cult of Artemis along the sea-board from Monaco to Barcelona. The name Marseilles derives from a Phoenician word for 'colony' and, although in actual historic sequence the Phocaeans displaced the Phoenicians as masters of the sea, in my text I put them in the same boat because they both were precursors of the Mediterranean thing in the lands of the Western seaboard.

55. In the Canon of Mass at the beginning of the prayer *Hanc igitur oblationem*, the rubric directs the priest to spread his hands over the offerings; and after the words 'that we be . . . counted within the flock of thy elect' a further rubric, *Jungit manus*, directs him to join his hands together.

56. What is pleaded in the Mass is precisely the argosy or voyage of the Redeemer, consisting of his entire sufferings and his death, his conquest of hades, his resurrection and his return in triumph to heaven. It is this that is offered to the Trinity (Cf. 'Myself to myself' as in the *Havamal* is said of Odin) on behalf of us argonauts and of the whole argosy of mankind, and, in some sense, of all sentient being, and, perhaps, of insentient too, for, as Paul says, 'The whole of nature, as we know, groans in a common travail all the while.' (Romans, viii, 22. Knox translation.)

57. Risings (or stringers) are pieces of timber running lengthways of a craft, into which the thwart-boards, on which the rowers sit, are fixed.

58. Cf. the Keys of Man; the sea-god Manannan (Manawydan) gave his name to that island; bearing also in mind the Keys of the Fisherman with the sword.

59. Land's End.

60. See note 46 to page 162 above.

From The Anathemata

Mabinog's Liturgy

1. It will be remembered that Helen's beauty was enhanced by the mole on her forehead and Aphrodite's by the cast in her eye. There was also the blemish in one eye of the British Venus, Emma Hamilton, which took 'nothing from her beauty'. And further that it was in the Ida range of mountains in Asia Minor that Aphrodite's offer was accepted above those of Hera or Athena and that perfection of form won the apple and not riches nor even success in battle. Paris' values were not at all bad. Further again, that only virgins can tame unicorns and that in some allegories the unicorn means our Lord.

2. Vanabride is Freyja. See note 18 to page 142 above.

3. By the European peoples, Greeks, Romans, Celts and Teutons, the wren, the smallest of birds, has been called the 'king of birds'. Frazer cites the Scottish folk-rhyme:

   > 'Malaisons, malaisons, mair than ten,
   > That harry the Ladye of Heaven's hen.'

4. See Dürer's painting the 'Virgin with the Irises'. The madonna is in a red dress with a purple cloak upon the paler purple lining of which a butterfly has alighted. From the Doughty House Collection, now in the National Gallery.

5. See pages 157 and 159 above.

6. Gwenhwyfar, gwen-hooy-varr, accent on middle syllable.

7. See *The Lady of the Fountain* '... more lovely than Gwenhwyfar the wife of Arthur, when she has appeared loveliest at the Offering, on the day of the Nativity or at the feast of Easter'. Guest's translation.

8. Calangaeaf, cal-an-gae-av, ae as ah+eh said quickly as a monosyllable. Winter-calends, November 1.

9. *Plygain*, plug-ein, ei as in height, dawn. This name is given to a Christmas observance when people assembled in the parish churches, lights being carried and carols sung. The hour varied, but in the eighteenth century it appears to have been at dawn. The many lights characterized this observance and it is the lights which are remembered. A church in Flintshire was burnt in 1532 and according to a nineteenth-century writer the fire was caused by the Plygain lights, 'in imitation of the High Mass, a custom particular to Wales'. As 1532 antedates the suppression of the Mass in Wales, this statement is very ambiguous, but it shows that the Plygain was *regarded* as a surrogate for something lost.

Notes

10. *Yntred*, Introit, un-tred, accent on first syllable. The *synaxis* (meeting) is that part of the Mass preceding the offertory prayer.

11. Strictly speaking the Mass essentially begins at the offertory prayer. In Welsh the Mass is called *Yr Offeren*, The Offering.

12. Cf. the thirteenth-century gloss on a MS of Nennius, which reads: 'Artur, translated into Latin, means *ursus horribilis*'. There is also the exceedingly obscure passage in Gildas where he calls some ruler Ursus, the Bear. There seems every reason for rejecting the suggestion that Gildas here refers to Arthur; but it may be noted that in Old Celtic the word for bear was *artos*, modern Welsh, *arth*.

13. Cf. the stuff called *gwellt troia*, 'Grass of Troy', mentioned by medieval Welsh poets, for example in c. 1450 'Grass of Troy like a maiden's hair, the Son's countenance in delicate embroidery', and in the same poem, *ystinos*, asbestos, is mentioned, 'A stone we know is spun come from great India to Gwent'. And in 1346 'Stockings of thin brilliantly-white asbestos; and this is what asbestos is—a precious brilliantly-white stone which is found in Farthest Spain, which can be spun'. And in 1520 'Bi-coloured sheen of Greek embroideries fit for nobles of the Round Table . . . a work of fire'. See F. G. Payne, *Guide to the Collection of Samplers and Embroideries*, Nat. Mus. of Wales, Cardiff, 1939.

14. Cf. the requiem mass for a woman deceased, '. . . on behalf of the soul of thy handmaid, N. etc.' and see Malory, Bk. XXI, on the obsequies of Guenever, 'And than she was wrapped in cered clothe of Raynes from the toppe to the too in thirtyfolde.'

15. Doleucothi (dol-ei-coth-ee, ei as in height, accent on third syllable) in Carmarthenshire, the only place in all Britain where gold was continuously mined in the Romano-British epoch. Many gold ornaments have also been discovered on the site.

16. Cf. 'At Llongborth saw I of Arthur's brave men hewing with steel (Men of the) emperor, director of toil', from a fragment in Early Welsh translated by the late John Rhŷs.

17. Those who have had occasion to move about in Forward Areas recall that it is possible, if disconcerting, to do so in bright full moonlight, provided that the moon is high in the sky.

18. Selenê and Helenê are so accented because the proper English forms, Selene and Helen, do not preserve the phonetic similarity of the two names, a similarity said to disclose a far more important mythological correspondence between Helen and the moon-goddess. See Jackson Knight, *Virgil's Troy*.

From The Anathemata

19. Owing to the success of the later Launcelot-Guenevere theme as a romance motif, the earlier, more basic and more political theme in the 'moste pyteuous tale of the morte Arthure saunz gwerdon' has been somewhat over-shadowed. I mean the destiny of Medraut (Mordred) 'For ys nat kynge Arthur youre uncle and no farther but youre modirs brothir and uppon hir he hymselffe begate you uppon his owne syster? Therefore how may ye wed youre owne fadirs wyff?' Malory, XXI, 1.

It seems not improbable that this Medraut theme contains elements of genuine historicity. It represents the tradition of a power-struggle in Britain between the *dux*, Artorius, and a group of his *equites*, during the forty years or so of peace that followed the halt of the Anglo-Saxon barbarians at the siege of Badon Hill. It fits in with what is known to the historians of the sub-Roman world. The intrigue involving the wife of Artorius in the traditional story is historically possible and such intrigue certainly fits in with the censures of Gildas against the British leaders a generation later.

20. In Welsh tradition one of Arthur's Gueneveres (there were three) was the daughter of Gogyrfan Gawr; the epithet *cawr* means 'giant', but it may also mean 'tyrant' in the sense used of Œdipus. *Cawraidd* is the adjectival form of *cawr* (*-aidd* as eith in either).

21. The *Notitia Dignitatum Imperii Romani* was an official compendium dealing with a variety of subjects from the dispositions of the defences of Britain to the number of lights carried before members of the imperial family. The Occidental section that has survived was issued early in the fifth century. While having this directory and book of etiquette in mind I am not citing a specific item.

22. Islont, iss-lont, accent on first syllable, called also Ynys-yr-la, Island of Snow, Iceland.

23. The Faeroe group.

24. *môrforwyn*, sea-maiden, mōrr-vorr-win, accent on the penultimate syllable. As has already been noted, Manawydan, man-now-wid-an, was a sea-god and perhaps an agriculture-god, who appears in the tales as a Welsh ruler with magical powers.

25. Thing-Ness, from thing (assembly) and ness (promontory). It has been suggested that there is a connection between this compound and the Welsh word for city, *dinas*, din-ass, accent on first syllable. Gynt, 'g' hard, from *gentes*, the Scandinavian peoples.

26. *hiraeth*, heer-aeth, ae as ah+eh, the Welsh word for yearning or longing, is also found in place-names as in the Hiraethog hills in Denbighshire,

Notes

and there is the theory that connects the word with a site-name envisaged in a Welsh-Scandinavian complex. In his book *Mabinogi Cymru* (1930) Mr Timothy Lewis gives a map showing a suggested cosmology of the world of the old tales and on it 'Hireth' is identified with Hordaland, now the district of South Bergenhus in Norway.

27. Demetia or Dyfed is South-West Wales.
    Cemeis, kem-ice, accent on first syllable.
    This ancient division of northern Pembrokeshire is said to be the home of much that went to the formation of the oldest legendary deposits.

28. Cf. the ballade, *Sir Patrick Spens*,
    'To Noroway o'er the faem' and 'And gurly grew the sea'.
    Cf. *brim* and *mere-flod*, for sea in O.E. and *mere-hengest*, sea-horse (mare) for ship. Friday or Frig's Day is Dydd Gwener in Welsh; Gwener from *Veneris*.

29. *Mabinogion*, mab-in-og-yon, accent on third syllable. The singular is *mabinogi* (mab-in-og-ee) the repertoire of a *mabinog* (accent on second syllable) a tyro bard; and meaning also a tale of infancy as in the tale called *Mabinogi Iesu Crist*. The root is *mab*, son, as in Maponus (Mabon) a Celtic god sometimes equated with Apollo.

30. Croglith, 'Lesson of the Cross'; crog-lith, accent on first syllable. In Wales Good Friday is called Dydd Gwener y Groglith, *crog*, cross, plus *llith* from *lectio*.

31. The word *bangor* means the top row of rods in a wattle fence. As the Celtic religious communities were enclosed in such fences the word appears to become applied in some cases to such enclosures. Cf. the place-names Bangor Iscoed, 'the *bangor* below the wood', and Bangor Fawr, 'the great *bangor*'.

32. *pared*, *a* as in parry, accent on first syllable. A dividing wall (from *parietem*), here meant of a chancel-screen.

33. Cf. The *Mabinogion*, where Manawydan practises the craft of cobbler and where Gwydion uses fungi as his medium which by transaccidentation he causes to have the appearance of richly harnessed horses. In Wales, as elsewhere, Virgil was associated with magic and so with alchemy, but in Wales today chemistry is still 'the art of Virgil' (*fferylliaeth*) and any chemist, Boots' Cash, is 'an agent of Virgil' (*fferyllydd*).
    Maridunum was the Roman name for Carmarthen, which is an anglicism for Caer-Fyrddin, which means Merlin's fort.

34. Cf., with regard to these clothes, the interesting examples, given by T. C. Lethbridge, of the probable influence of the Classical forms on the

From The Anathemata

Celtic and Teutonic peoples, even those outside the Roman world, and as late as the Norse-Irish wars. (See *Merlin's Island*, 144–145.)

35. *Lacerna, paenula, planeta, phelonion, amphibalum, casula*, in Welsh *casul*, in English chasuble, by whatever name, this rational, probably Ionian, garment became increasingly fashionable in the Roman world from the third century and was still worn in the seventh century; to be subsequently retained by the conservatism of the Church, so that clergy still wore it in 1950, but now only if they are priests and only at Mass and only if they are celebrants of the Mass. When these, who alone are now privileged to wear it, kiss it and put it on, perhaps they sometimes remember that had not Roman, sub-Roman and post-Roman persons of various sorts and their wives and daughters worn it as a customary top-coat, they would not now be wearing it as the specific sign of those who represent rational man and who offer a rational sacrifice under the forms of bread and wine. About 400 the chasuble was compulsory for senators, and in a contemporary painting (cited by Duchesne), Gregory the Great (540–604), his father *and his mother* are each wearing it.

36. Cf. the purple chasuble embroidered with golden bees, worn at Byzantium as the exclusive prerogative of the imperial house. Caer Gustennin, keirr, ei as in height, gis-tén-nin; Constantinople.

37. Three linen cloths, one over the other, are used to dress a Christian altar. During the action of the Mass a further piece of linen is spread centrally and on this the chalice and paten are placed. Cf. the older method of covering the chalice with part of this linen cloth (corporal), a use still followed by the Carthusians at Cowfold and I suppose by them elsewhere.

38. Cf. Loidis Regio or Elmete, the British district in the West Riding. In my text the name 'Loidis' must be taken symbolically of any pocket of resistance in times of confused and shifting frontiers; I am not implying that 'Ilkley moor' was in fact grain-producing.

39. Cf. Nial of the Nine Hostages (whose last raid in the Severn area may possibly have been the occasion of the carrying off of the future St Patrick), and such-like Irish raiders who, during the fourth, fifth and sixth centuries, were to the west of Britain what Saxons were to the east and Picts to the north.

40. The ref. here is to Spengler's terms, 'Magian culture' and 'Apollinian culture'. The manual act of consecration in the Mass is of the former culture, while the words of consecration are generally in a language of the latter.

Notes

41. Anamnesis. I take leave to remind the reader that this is a key-word in our deposits. The dictionary defines its general meaning as 'the recalling of things past'. But what is the nature of this particular recalling? I append the following quotation as being clear and to the point: 'It (anamnesis) is not quite easy to represent accurately in English, words like "remembrance" or "memorial" having for us a connotation of something *absent* which is only mentally recollected. But in the scriptures of both the Old and New Testament *anamnesis* and the cognate verb have a sense of "recalling" or "re-presenting" before God an event in the past so that it becomes *here and now operative by its effects*'. Gregory Dix, *The Shape of the Liturgy*, p. 161.

42. 'We find an Egyptian king claiming in his coffin-text his identification with Osiris and adding "I am barley".' Eliot Smith, *Human History*, p. 281.

43. *boneddigion*, bon-eth-ig-yon, th as in nether, accent on penultimate syllable, from *bonedd*, descent. The term is borrowed here from the Welsh laws of the early middle ages, it meant free-born men, and is often qualified by the adjective *cynhwynol*, innate. Today it has the less precise meaning of 'gentlemen'.

44. *Qui pridie*, the opening words of the prayer of Institution in the Mass 'Who, the day before he suffered, etc.' It is during this prayer that the words of consecration are said, followed by the showing of the sacrament to the people.

BEIRD·BYT·BARNANT
the bards of the world assess
WYR·O·GALLON
the men of valour: but
SVPER·SELLAM·IVDICIS
NON·SEDEBVNT:
SED·CREATVRAM·ÆVI
CONFIRMABVNT
ET·DEPRECATIO·ILLO
RVM·IN·OPERA
TIONE·ARTIS
and without these: non ædificatur civitas

FROM

The Sleeping Lord
and other fragments

THE TRIBUNE'S VISITATION

Sir!
No sir, yes sir, Middle Watch Relief, sir.
Just come off, sir.
Yes sir.
Well, no sir, half an hour back, sir.
No sir, some from last levy
                    some, redrafted.
No sir, from all parts, sir.
In particular?
I see, and you, sergeant?
The Urbs, sir, Regio 4, sir.
Fifteen years, sir, come next October Games.

October Games!
                    and whose games, pray, are these?
Some Judy-show
                    to make the flowers grow?
the April mocked man
                    crowned and cloaked
I suppose
                    going rustic are they[1]
                    under y'r very nose
and you good Cockney bred
born well in sound of the geese-cry
and with the Corona up, I see
                    and of the First Grade.
Where won? or was it an issue, sergeant?
On the German *limes*, sir.

From The Sleeping Lord and other fragments

And y'r bar?
On the German *limes*, sir, North Sector.
And the two torques?
On the same *limes*, sir, South Sub-Sector, sir, in front of Fosse 60, sir, the other . . .

Enough! I'm not asking for back-filed awards or press *communiqués*—no doubt the *Acta*[2] gave you half a column on how plebeian blood's no bar to bravery—I know it all and backwards. But we'll speak presently, you and I.
                      For now, where's this mixed bunch
of yours?
                                I have a word to say.

Yes sir, very good sir, Guard! Guard!
for inspection . . .
Cease man, cease!
                    A liturgy too late
is best not sung.
                    Stand them at ease
                    stand them easy
let each of you stand each as you are
let these sleep on and take their rest
                    if any man can sleep
to equinoctial runes
                    and full-moon incantations.

You, corporal, stand yourself easy.
You, whose face I seem to know
                    a good Samnite face.
Private what? Pontius what?
A rare name too, for trouble.

And you with the Etruscan look
not Pte Maecenas by any chance?
No sir, 330099 Elbius, sir.

The Tribune's Visitation

But with a taste for the boards, eh? We must remember that at the reg'mental binge. That lorica back to front and y'r bared flanks become you well—extremely funny and very like your noble ancestors, unless the terracotta lies.

But all of you stand
                        I have a word to say.
First, a routine word
                    a gloss on the book
and no more, a sergeant's word—sergeant.

Men, when you are dismissed to quarters, it is to quarter-duties, not to Saturnalia. The regulation rest's allowed, now get on to those kits, on to those brasses. D'you think that steel's brought from Toletum at some expense for you to let to rust—and those back-rivets and under those frogs . . .
    but must I do a corporal's nagging, must I be scold, like a second cook to pallid sluts beneath her, must I read out a rooky's list of do's and don'ts and speak of overlaps and where to buy metal-polish. Are there no lance-jacks to demonstrate standing orders?
                    Does the legate need to do
what he delegates?
                      Must those with curial charge
be ever prying on a swarm of vicars
                      or nothing goes forward?
Must tribunes bring gunfire[3] to centurions or else there's no parade?

But enough: analogies are wearisome and I could analogise to the end of time, my Transpadane grandma's friend taught me the tricks. I'd beat the rhetoric of Carnutic conjurors and out-poet ovates from druid bangors farside the Gaulish Strait. But I'll be

From The Sleeping Lord and other fragments

'forthright Roman' as the saying goes, but seldom goes beyond the saying. Let's fit our usage to the tag—for once.

The loricas of Caesar's men
                    should shine like Caesar
                    back and front
whose thorax shines all ways
                    and to all quarters
                    to the world-ends
whether he face unstable Britain
                    or the weighty Persians.
So that all of them say:
                    Rome's back is never turned.

But a word more: this chitty's fire is built for section's rations, not for warming backsides. Is Jerusalem on Caucasus? Are your Roman loins so starved that Caledonian trews were best indented for? Should all the aunts on Palatine knit you Canusian comforts, or shall we skin the bear of Lebanon and mount the guard in muffs?

Come! leave that chatter and that witch-wife song, that charcoal can well tend itself; now do you attend your several duties.

Guard, guard—at ease! Guard! . . .
No, sergeant, no, not so anxious
                    I have a word to say
I have a more necessary word.
I would bring you to attention
                    not liturgically
                    but in actuality.

The Tribune's Visitation

The legate has spoken of a misplaced objectivity. I trust a serving officer may know both how to be objective and to judge the time and place. For me the time is now and here the place.

You sergeant, you junior N.C.O.s
                                my order was stand easy
men less at ease I've seldom seen.

It belongs to the virtue of rank to command. If I, by virtue of my rank, deem it necessary to command composure, then compose yourselves. I have a word to say for which a measure of composure may, in you, be requisite.

                      I have a word to say to you as men and as a man speaking to men, but, and a necessary but, as a special sort of man speaking to a special sort of men at a specific but recurring moment in *urbs*-time.

Is this a hut on Apennine, where valley-gossips munch the chestnuts and croak Saturnian spells? Is this how guard-details stand by for duties who guard the world-utilities?

Old rhyme, no doubt, makes beautiful
                            the older fantasies
but leave the stuff
                        to the men in skirts
who beat the bounds
                        of small localities
all that's done with
                        for the likes of us
in *Urbs*, throughout *orbis*.

From The Sleeping Lord and other fragments

It's not the brotherhood of the fields or the Lares of a remembered hearth, or the consecrated wands bending in the fertile light to transubstantiate for child-man the material vents and flows of nature into the breasts and milk of the goddess.

                    Suchlike bumpkin sacraments
are for the young-time
                    for the dream-watches
now we serve contemporary fact.

                  It's the world-bounds
we're detailed to beat
                  to discipline the world-floor
to a common level
                  till everything presuming difference
and all the sweet remembered demarcations
                  wither
to the touch of us
                  and know the fact of empire.
Song? antique song
                  from known-site
spells remembered from the breast?
                  No!

But Latin song, you'll say, good song the fathers sang, the aboriginal and variant alliterations known to each small *pagus*. The remembered things of origin and streamhead, the things of the beginnings, of our own small beginnings.

                  The loved parts of that whole
which, when whole
                  subdued to wholeness
all the world.

The Tribune's Visitation

These several streams, these local growths, all that belongs to the fields of Latium, to the Italic fatherland, surely these things, these dear pieties, should be remembered?

It stands to reason you'll say, these things, deep things, integral to ourselves, make for efficiency, steady the reg'mental will, make the better men, the better soldiers, so the better friends of Caesar.

               No, not so
that pretty notion, too, must go.
                   Only the neurotic
look to their beginnings.

We are men of now and must strip as the facts of now would have it. Step from the caul of fantasy even if it be the fantasy of sweet Italy.
Spurn the things of Saturn's Tellus?
Yes, if memory of them
                   (some pruned and bearing tree
                   our sister's song)
calls up some embodiment
                   of early loyalty
raises some signum
                   which, by a subconscious trick
softens the edge of our world intention.

Now listen: Soldiers, comrades and brothers, men of the Cohors Italica, men of my command, guard-details, I address you.

I've never been one for the vine-stick, I've never been a

From The Sleeping Lord and other fragments

sergeant-major 'Hand-us-Another'[4] to any man. We can do without a Lucilius in this mob, but we want no Vibulenuses neither.

I would speak as Caesar's friend to Caesar's friends. I would say my heart, for I am in a like condemnation.

I too could weep
                    for these Saturnian spells
and for the remembered things.
                If you are Latins
so am I.

If the glowing charcoals draw your hearts to braziers far from this parched Judaean wall, does it not so draw my heart?

                If the sour issue tot
hardly enough to wet the whistle
yet calls up in each of you
                some remembered fuller cup
                from Luna vats
do not I too remember cups so filled
                among companions?
                the brews of known-site
                and the vintage hymn
within a white enclosure
                our side Our Sea?
No dying Gaul
                figures in the rucked circus sand
his far green valley
                more clear than do I figure
from this guard-house door
                a little porch below Albanus.

The Tribune's Visitation

No grave Teuton of the Agrippian *ala* rides to death on stifling marl-banks, where malarial Jordan falls to the Dead Meer, thinking of broad salubrious Rhine, more tenderly than do I think of mudded Tiber.

And we've lesser streams than Tiber
                        and more loved
more loved because more known
                        more known
because our mothers' wombs
                        were opened on their margins
and our sisters' shifts
                        laved in the upper pools
and pommelled snowy
                        on the launder-banks.

These tributary streams we love so well make confluence with Tiber and Tiber flows to Ostia and is lost in the indifferent sea.

But Our Sea, you'll say, still *our* sea—you raise the impatient shout, still the Roman Sea, that bears up all the virtues of the Middle World, is tideless and constant, bringing the norm, without variation, to the several shores.

                      Are you party members
doped with your own propaganda?

Or poets who must need weave dreams and yet more dreams, saleable dreams, to keep the duns from doorstep, or have hearts as doting as those elder ministers who think the race of gods wear togas?

From The Sleeping Lord and other fragments

                But you are soldiers
with no need for illusion
             for, willy-nilly
you must play the appointed part . . .
Listen! be silent!
                you *shall* understand
the horror of this thing.
Dear brothers, sweet men, Italian loves
              it may not be.

We speak of ends and not of origins when Tiber flows by Ostia. The place is ill-named, for mouths receive to nourish bodies, but here the maw of the world sucks down all the variant sweets of Mother Italy and drains to world-sea the blessed differences: No longer the Veneti, no more Campanian, not the Samnite summer pipes nor the Apulian winter song, not the Use of Lanuvium nor the *Etrusca disciplina*, not Vetulonia of the iron fasces, not the Ayra of Praeneste in the gold fibulas, nor any of the things of known-site . . .

              our world-Maristuran
marshals all to his world-sea.

Bucinator Taranus, swilling his quarter's pay with his Combrogean listing-mates, tough Lugobelinus and the radiant Maponus[5] (an outlandish triad to wear the Roman lorica), maudlin in their barrack cups habitually remember some high hill-cymanfa; thus our canteens echo with:

      '*No more in dear Orddwy
      We drink the dear meddlyn*'[6]

or some such dolorous anamnesis.

Now we, for whom their Ordovician hills are yet outside the

The Tribune's Visitation

world (but shortly to be levelled to the world-plain) must think no more of our dear sites or brews of this dear *pagus*, or that known enclosure loved of Pales, lest, thinking of our own, our bowels turn when we are commanded to storm the palisades of others and the world-plan be undone by plebeian pity.

As wine of the country
                        sweet if drawn from wood
near to the living wood
                        that bore the grape
                        sours if taken far
so can all virtue curdle in transit
so vice may be virtue uprooted
so is the honey-root of known-site
                        bitter fruit for world-floor.

The cultural obsequies must be already sung before empire can masquerade a kind of life.

What! does Caesar mime?
                        are the world-boards his stage?
Do we, his actors, but mimic for a podium full of jeering gods what once was real?

That seems about the shape of it, O great Autocrator, whose commission I hold, but hold it I do, over and above the *sacramentum* that binds us all.

What then?
                        Are we the ministers of death?
                        of life-in-death?

From The Sleeping Lord and other fragments

do we but supervise the world-death
                         being dead ourselves
long since?

Do we but organize the extension of death whose organisms withered with the old economies behind the living fences of the small localities?

Men of my command, guard details of the Antonia, soldiers of our Greater Europa, saviours of our world-hegemony, tiros or veterans, whichever you be, I have called you brothers, and so you are, I am your elder brother and would speak and command fraternally.

Already I have said enough to strip me of my office, but comrades, I did so from a full heart, from a bursting heart and knowing your hearts . . .

                       but set the doors to
let's stand within
                       and altogether
let's shut out
                       the prying dawn

I have things to say
                       not for the world-wind to bear away
but for your ears, alone, to hear.
                       I have spoken from a burning heart
I speak now more cool
                       (if even less advised)
within these guard-house walls
                       which do, here and for us
enclose our home

The Tribune's Visitation

                and we one family of one *gens*
and I the *pater familias*
                these standards, the *penates*
however shorn to satisfy
                the desert taboos
                of jealous baals.

This chitty's fire, our paternal hearth, these fatigue-men our sisters, busy with the pots, so then, within this sacred college we can speak *sub rosa* and the rose that seals our confidence is that red scar that shines on the limbs of each of us who have the contact with the fire of Caesar's enemies, and if on some of us that sear burns, then on all, on you tiros no less than on these *veterani*
                for all are members
of the Strider's body.
                And if not of one hope
then of one necessity.
For we all are attested to one calling
not any more several, but one.
And one to what purpose?
                and by what necessity?

See! I break this barrack bread, I drink with you, this issue cup, I salute, with you, these mutilated signa, I with you have cried with all of us the ratifying formula: *Idem in me.*

                So, if the same oath serve
why, let the same illusions fall away.

Let the gnosis of necessity infuse our hearts, for we have purged out the leaven of illusion.

From The Sleeping Lord and other fragments

If then we are dead to nature
                yet we live
                to Caesar
                from Caesar's womb we issue
by a second birth.

Ah! Lucina!
                what irradiance
can you bring
                to this parturition?
What light brights this deliverance?
From darkness
                to a greater dark
the issue is.

Sergeant, that shall serve, for now.

THE TUTELAR OF THE PLACE

She that loves place, time, demarcation, hearth, kin, enclosure, site, differentiated cult, though she is but one mother of us all: one earth brings us all forth, one womb receives us all, yet to each she is other, named of some name other . . .

. . . other sons, beyond hill, over strath, or never so neighbouring by nigh field or near crannog up stream. What co-tidal line can plot if nigrin or flax-head marching their wattles be cognate or german of common totem?

Tellus of the myriad names answers to but one name: From this tump she answers Jac o' the Tump only if he call Great-Jill-of-the-tump-that-bare-me, not if he cry by some new fangle moder of far gentes over the flud, fer-goddes name from anaphora of far folk wont woo her; she's a rare one for locality. Or, gently she bends her head from far-height when tongue-strings chime the name she whispered on known-site, as between sister and brother at the time of beginnings . . . when the wrapped bands are cast and the worst mewling is over, after the weaning and before the august initiations, in the years of becoming.
When she and he 'twixt door-stone and fire-stane prefigure and puppet on narrow floor-stone the world-masque on wide world-floor.
When she attentively changes her doll-shift, let's pretend with solemnity as rocking the womb-gift.
When he chivvies house-pet with his toy *hasta*, makes believe the cat o' the wold falls to the pitiless bronze.

From The Sleeping Lord and other fragments

         Man-travail and woman-war here we see enacted are.
      When she and he beside the settle, he and she between the trestle-struts, mime the bitter dance to come.
Cheek by chin at the childer-crock where the quick tears drop and the quick laughter dries the tears, within the rim of the shared curd-cup each fore-reads the world-storm.
Till the spoil-sport gammers sigh:
         Now come on now little children, come on now it's past the hour. Sun's to roost, brood's in pent, dusk-star tops mound, lupa sniffs the lode-damps for stragglers late to byre.
Come now it's time to come now for tarry awhile and slow
      cot's best for yeanlings
      crib's best for babes
here's a rush to light you to bed
here's a fleece to cover your head
against the world-storm
    brother by sister
under one *brethyn*
kith of the kin warmed at the one hearth-flame
(of the seed of far-gaffer? fair gammer's wer-gifts?)
cribbed in garth that the garth-Jill wards.

Though she inclines with attention from far fair-height outside all boundaries, beyond the known and kindly nomenclatures, where all names are one name, where all stones of demarcation dance and interchange, troia the skipping mountains, nod recognitions.
As when on known-site ritual frolics keep bucolic interval at eves and divisions when they mark the inflexions of the year and conjugate with trope and turn the season's syntax, with beating feet, with wands and pentagons to spell out the Trisagion.

The Tutelar of the Place

Who laud and magnify with made, mutable and beggarly elements the unmade immutable begettings and precessions of fair-height, with halting sequences and unresolved rhythms, searchingly, with what's to hand, under the inconstant lights that hover world-flats, that bright by fit and start the tangle of world-wood, rifting the dark drifts for the wanderers that wind the world-meander, who seek hidden grammar to give back anathema its first benignity.
Gathering all things in, twining each bruised stem to the swaying trellis of the dance, the dance about the sawn lode-stake on the hill where the hidden stillness is at the core of struggle, the dance around the green lode-tree on far fair-height where the secret guerdons hang and the bright prizes nod, where sits the queen *im Rosenhage* eating the honey-cake, where the king sits, counting-out his man-geld, rhyming the audits of all the world-holdings.

Where the marauder leaps the wall and the wall dances to the marauder's leaping, where the plunging wolf-spear and the wolf's pierced diaphragm sing the same song . . .

Yet, when she stoops to hear you children cry
        from the scattered and single habitations
or from the nucleated holdings
              from tower'd *castra*
              paved *civitas*
              treble-ramped *caer*
              or wattled *tref*
                    stockaded *gorod* or
                    trenched *burh*
from which ever child-crib within whatever enclosure
demarked by a dynast or staked by consent
wherever in which of the wide world-ridings
        you must not call her but by that name
which accords to the morphology of that place.

From The Sleeping Lord and other fragments

Now pray now little children for us all now, pray our gammer's
prayer according to our *disciplina* given to us
within our labyrinth on our dark mountain.
      Say now little children:
Sweet Jill of our hill hear us
bring slow bones safe at the lode-ford
keep lupa's bite without our wattles
make her bark keep children good
save us all from dux of far folk
save us from the men who plan.
Now sleep on, little children, sleep on now, while I tell out the
greater suffrages, not yet for young heads to understand:

Queen of the differentiated sites, administratrix of the demarca-
tions, let our cry come unto you.
      In all times of imperium save us when the
mercatores come save us
   from the guile of the *negotiatores* save us from the *missi*,
from the agents
     who think no shame
by inquest to audit what is shameful to tell
        deliver us.
When they check their capitularies in their curias
      confuse their reckonings.
When they narrowly assess the *trefydd*
      by hide and rod
      by *pentan* and pent
by impost and fee on beast-head
      and roof-tree
and number the souls of men
     notch their tallies false
disorder what they have collated.
When they proscribe the diverse uses and impose the
rootless uniformities, pray for us.
      When they sit in *Consilium*

The Tutelar of the Place

to liquidate the holy diversities
                  mother of particular perfections
                  queen of otherness
                  mistress of asymmetry
patroness of things counter, parti, pied, several
protectress of things known and handled
help of things familiar and small
                  wardress of the secret crevices
                of things wrapped and hidden
mediatrix of all the deposits
                margravine of the troia
empress of the labyrinth
                receive our prayers.
When they escheat to the Ram
                        in the Ram's curia
the seisin where the naiad sings
                above where the forked rod bends
or where the dark outcrop
            tells on the hidden seam
pray for the green valley.
When they come with writs of oyer and terminer
                to hear the false and
                    determine the evil
according to the advices of the Ram's magnates who serve the
Ram's wife, who write in the Ram's book of Death.
In the bland megalopolitan light
     where no shadow is by day or by night
be our shadow.
Remember the mound-kin, the kith of the *tarren* gone from this
mountain because of the exorbitance of the Ram . . . remember
them in the rectangular tenements, in the houses of the engines
that fabricate the ingenuities of the Ram . . . Mother of Flowers
save them then where no flower blows.
                      Though they shall not come again
because of the requirements of the Ram with respect to the world
plan, remember them where the dead forms multiply, where no

From The Sleeping Lord and other fragments

stamen leans, where the carried pollen falls to the adamant surfaces, where is no crevice.
In all times of *Gleichschaltung*, in the days of the central economies, set up the hedges of illusion round some remnant of us, twine the wattles of mist, white-web a Gwydion-hedge
    like fog on the *bryniau*
    against the commissioners
and assessors bearing the writs of the Ram to square the world-floor and number the tribes and write down the secret things and take away the diversities by which we are, by which we call on your name, sweet Jill of the demarcations
    arc of differences
    tower of individuation
    queen of the minivers
laughing in the mantle of variety
belle of the mound
    for Jac o'the mound
our belle and donnabelle
    on all the world-mountain.
In the December of our culture ward somewhere the secret seed, under the mountain, under and between, between the grids of the Ram's survey when he squares the world-circle.
Sweet Mair devise a mazy-guard
in and out and round about
double-dance defences
countermure and echelon meanders round
the holy mound
    fence within the fence
pile the dun ash for the bright seed
    (within the curtained wood the canister
within the canister the budding rod)
troia in depth the shifting wattles of illusion for the ancilia for the palladia for the kept memorials, because of the commissioners of the Ram and the Ram's decree concerning the utility of the hidden things.

The Tutelar of the Place

When the technicians manipulate the dead limbs of our culture as though it yet had life, have mercy on us. Open unto us, let us enter a second time within your stola-folds in those days— ventricle and refuge both, *hendref* for world-winter, asylum from world-storm. Womb of the Lamb the spoiler of the Ram.

c. 1960 incorporating passages written earlier

THE HUNT

              . . . and the hundreds and twenties
of horsed *palatini*
              (to each *comitatus*
one Penteulu)
              that closely hedge
              with a wattle of weapons
the firsts among equals
              from the wattled *palasau*
the torqued *arglwyddi*
              of calamitous jealousy[1]
(if there were riders from the Faithful Fetter-locked War-Band there were riders also from the Three Faithless War-Bands: the riders who receive the shaft-shock
              in place of their radiant lords
the riders who slip the column
              whose lords alone
              receive the shafts)[2]
    when the men of proud spirit and the men of mean spirit, the named and the unnamed of the Island and the name-bearing steeds of the Island and the dogs of the Island and the silent lords and the lords of loud mouth, the leaders of familiar visage from the dear known-sites and the adjuvant stranger lords with aid for the hog-hunt from over the Sleeve[3]
    and the wand-bearing lords that are kin to Fferyllt[4] (who learned from the Sibyl the Change Date and the Turn of Time) the lords who ride after deep consideration and the lords whose inveterate habit is to ride the riders who ride from interior compulsion and the riders who fear the narrow glances of the kindred.

The Hunt

Those who would stay for the dung-bailiff's daughter and those who would ride though the shining *matres* three by three sought to stay them.[5]

The riders who would mount though the green wound unstitched and those who would leave their mounts in stall if the bite of a gadfly could excuse them.

The innate Combroges,[6] by father by mother without mixed without brok'n without mean descent, all the lords from among the co-equals and the quasi-free of limited privilege, whose insult price is unequal but whose limb-price is equal for all the disproportion as to comeliness and power because the dignity belonging to the white limbs and innate in the shining members, annuls inequality of status and disallows distinctions of appearance.[7]

When the free and the bond and the mountain mares and the fettled horses and the four-penny curs and the hounds of status in the wide, jewelled collars
               when all the shining Arya[8] rode
with the diademed leader
          who directs the toil
          whose face is furrowed
with the weight of the enterprise
   the lord of the conspicious scars whose visage is fouled with the hog-spittle whose cheeks are fretted with the grime of the hunt-toil:
              if his forehead is radiant
like the smooth hill in the lateral light
             it is corrugated
like the defences of the hill
             because of his care for the land
and for the men of the land.

If his eyes are narrowed for the stress of the hunt and because of the hog they are moist for the ruin and for love of the recumbent bodies that strew the ruin.

If his embroidered habit is clearly from a palace wardrobe it is mired and rent and his bruised limbs gleam from between the

From The Sleeping Lord and other fragments

rents, by reason of the excessive fury of his riding when he rode the close thicket as though it were an open launde
                 (indeed, was it he riding the forest-ride or was the tangled forest riding?)
    for the thorns and flowers of the forest and the bright elm-shoots and the twisted tanglewood of stamen and stem clung and meshed him and starred him with variety
    and the green tendrils gartered him and briary-loops galloon him with splinter-spike and broken blossom twining his royal needlework
                 and ruby petal-points counter
the countless points of his wounds
    and from his lifted cranium where the priced tresses dragged with sweat stray his straight brow-furrows under the twisted diadem
                 to the numbered bones
of his scarred feet
                 and from the saturated forelock
of his maned mare
                 to her streaming flanks
and in broken festoons for her quivering fetlocks
he was caparison'd in the flora
                 of the woodlands of Britain
and like a stricken numen of the woods
                 he rode
with the trophies of the woods
                 upon him
who rode
                 for the healing of the woods
and because of the hog.
    Like the breast of the cock-thrush that is torn in the hedge-war when bright on the native mottle the deeper mottling is and brighting the diversity of textures and crystal-bright on the delicate fret the clear dew-drops gleam: so was his dappling and his dreadful variety
                 the speckled lord of Prydain

The Hunt

in his twice-embroidered coat
                      the bleeding man in the green
and if through the trellis of green
                      and between the rents of the needlework
the whiteness of his body shone
                      so did his dark wounds glisten.

    And if his eyes, from their scrutiny of the hog-track and from considering the hog, turned to consider the men of the host (so that the eyes of the men of the host met his eyes) it would be difficult to speak of so extreme a metamorphosis.
                      When they paused at the check
when they drew breath.
    And the sweat of the men of the host and of the horses salted the dew of the forest-floor and the hard-breathing of the many men and of the many dogs and of the horses woke the fauna-cry of the Great Forest[9] and shook the silent flora.
                      And the extremity of anger
alternating with sorrow
                      on the furrowed faces
of the Arya
                      transmogrified the calm face
of the morning
                      as when the change-wind stirs
and the colours change in the boding thunder-calm
                      because this was the Day
of the Passion of the Men of Britain
                      when they hunted the Hog
life for life.

c. 1964 incorporating passages written c. 1950 or earlier

From

THE SLEEPING LORD

* * *

So then, whether seated
     at this board in his hall
or lying on his sleep-board
     in his lime whited *ystafell*[1]
with his bed-coverlet over him to cover him
     a work of the Chief Stitching Maid
to Yr Arglwyddes[2] (his, the Bear's wife)
of many vairs of stitched together
     marten-cat pelts
contrived without visible seam
     from the top throughout.

     Or, here, out
on the cold, open *moelion*[3]
     his only coverlet
his madder-dyed war-*sagum*
     where he slumbers awhile
from the hunt-toil:
     carried lights
     for the lord
in his pillar'd basilica
     carried lights
     for the lord
fain to lie down
     in the hog-wasted *blaendir*[4]
scorch-marks only

From The Sleeping Lord

                where were the white dwellings:
stafell[5] of the lord of the Cantref
                ys tywyll heno
shieling of the *taeog*[6] from the bond-tref
                heb dan, heb wely.[7]
And the trees of the *llannerch*?[8]
                Why are they fallen?
What of the *llwyn*[9] where the fair *onnen*[10] grew and the silvery queen of the *coedwig*[11] (as tough as she's graced & slender) that whispers her secrets low to the divining hazel, and the resistant oak boughs that antler'd dark above the hornbeam?

                Incedunt arbusta per alta
                    rapacibus caedunt
                Percellunt sacras quercus . . .
                Fraxinus frangitur . . .[12]

Not by long-hafted whetted steel axe-blades
                are these fallen
that graced the high slope
                that green-filigreed
the green hollow
                but by the riving tusks
of the great hog
                are they felled.
It is the Boar Trwyth[13]
                that has pierced through
the stout-fibred living wood
                that bears the sacral bough of gold.
    It is the hog that has ravaged the fair *onnen* and the hornbeam and the Queen of the Woods. It is the hog that has tusk-riven the tendoned roots of the trees of the *llwyn* whereby are the tallest with the least levelled low and lie up-so-down.
    It is the great *ysgithrau*[14] of the *porcus Troit* that have stove in the wattled walls of the white dwellings, it is he who has stamped out the seed of fire, shattered the *pentan*[15]-stone within

From The Sleeping Lord and other fragments

the dwellings; strewn the green leaf-bright limbs with the broken white limbs of the folk of the dwellings, so that the life-sap of the flowers of the forest mingles the dark life-sap of the fair bodies of the men who stood in the trackway of the long tusked great hog, *y twrch dirfawr ysgithrog hir*.[16]

Tawny-black sky-scurries
                low over
Ysgyryd[17] hill
and over the level-topped heights
                of Mynnydd Pen-y-fal[18]
                cold is wind
                grey is rain, but
                BRIGHT IS CANDELA
where this lord is in slumber.

Are his wounded ankles
                lapped with the ferric waters
that all through the night
                hear the song
from the night-dark seams
                where the narrow-skulled *caethion*[19]
labour the changing shifts
                for the cosmocrats of alien lips
in all the fair lands
                of the dark measures under
(from about Afon Lwyd
                in the confines of green Siluria
westward to where the naiad of the *fons*-head
                pours out the Lesser Gwendraeth[20]
high in the uplands
                above Ystrad Tywi[21]
and indeed further
                west & south of Merlin's Caer
even in the lost cantrevs
                of spell-held Demetia

From The Sleeping Lord

where was Gorsedd Arberth,[22] where the *palas*[23] was
                      where the prince who hunted
met the Prince of Hunters
                      in his woof of grey
and gleam-pale dogs
                      not kennelled on earth-floor
lit the dim chase.)

Is the Usk a drain for his gleaming tears
who weeps for the land
                      who dreams his bitter dream
for the folk of the land
does Tawe[24] clog for his sorrows
do the parallel dark-seam drainers
                      mingle his anguish-stream
with the scored valleys' tilted refuse.
Does his freight of woe
                      flood South by East
on Sirhywi[25] and Ebwy[26]
                      is it southly bourn
on double Rhondda's fall to Taff?[27]

  Do the stripped boughs grapple
above the troubled streams
                      when he dream-fights
his nine-day's fight
                      which he fought alone
with the hog in the Irish wilderness
                      when the eighteen twilights
                      and the ten midnights
and the equal light of the nine mid-mornings
were equally lit
                      with the light of the saviour's fury
and the dark fires of the hog's eye
which encounter availed him nothing.

From The Sleeping Lord and other fragments

                    Is his royal anger ferriaged
where black-rimed Rhymni
             soils her Marcher-banks
             Do the bells of St. Mellon's
toll his dolour
                are his sighs canalled
where the mountain-ash
              droops her bright head
for the black pall of Merthyr?

Do Afan[28] and Nedd[29] west it away
does grimed Ogwr[30] toss on a fouled ripple
his broken-heart flow
              out to widening Hafren[31]
            and does she, the Confluence Queen
queenly bear on her spume-frilled frock
a maimed king's sleep bane?
             Do the long white hands
would you think, of the Brides of the Déssi
            unloose galloons
to let the black tress-stray
            web the pluvial Westerlies
does the vestal flame in virid-hilled Kildare
            renew from secret embers
the undying fire
             that sinks on the Hill Capitoline
  Does the wake-dole mingle the cormorant scream
does man-*sídhe* to fay-queen bemoan
the passage of a king's griefs, westing far
             out to moon-swayed Oceanus
  Does the blind & unchoosing creature of sea know the marking and indelible balm from flotsomed sewage and the seaped valley-waste?
  Does the tide-beasts' maw
             drain down the princely tears

From The Sleeping Lord

with the mullocked slag-wash
                of Special Areas?
Can the tumbling and gregarious porpoises
does the aloof and infrequent seal
                that suns his puckered back
                and barks from Pirus' rock
tell the dole-tally of a drowned *taeog* from a
Gwledig's golden collar, refracted in Giltar shoal?

  Or, is the dying gull
                on her sea-hearse
that drifts the oily bourne
                to tomb at turn of tide
her own stricken cantor?
Or is it for the royal tokens
                that with her drift
that the jagg'd and jutting *morben*[32] echoes
and the deep hollows of *yr ogof*[33] echo
and the hollow eddies echo:
                Dirige, dirige[34]
and out, far, far beyond
on thalassic Brendan's heaving trackway
to unknown *insulae*
                where they sing
their west In Paradisums[35]
                and the corposants toss
for the dying flax-flame
                and West-world glory
in transit is.

But yet he sleeps:
                when he shifts a little in his fitful
slumber does a covering stone dislodge
                and roll to Reynoldstone?
When he fretfully turns

From The Sleeping Lord and other fragments

      crying out in a great voice
      in his fierce sleep-anger
does the habergeon'd sentinel
     alert himself sudden
from his middle-watch doze
      in the crenelled traverse-bay
of the outer bailey wall
      of the *castell*[36] these Eingl-Ffrancwyr[37]
call in their lingua La Haie Taillée
that the Saeson[38] other ranks
     call The Hay
(which place is in the tongue of the men of the land,
Y Gelli Gandryll, or, for short, Y Gelli)

Does he cock his weather-ear, enquiringly
lest what's on the west wind
      from over beyond the rising contours
may signify that in the broken
     tir y blaenau[39]
these broken dregs of Troea
     yet again muster?
Does he nudge his drowsing mate?
     Do the pair of them
say to each other: 'Twere not other
than wind-cry, for sure—yet
     best to warn the serjeant below.
He'll maybe
     warn the Captain of the Watch
or some such
     and he, as like as not
may think best to rouse the Castellan
     —that'll please him
in his newly glazed, arras-hung chamber
     with his Dean-coal fire
nicely blazing

From The Sleeping Lord

snug with his dowsabel
                        in the inner keep
Wont improve his temper, neither, come the morrow
with this borough and hereabouts alerted
                        and all for but a wind-bluster.
Still, you never know, so
                        best stand on Standing Orders
and report to them as has the serjeancy
the ordering and mandate, for
you never know, mate:
                        wind-stir may be, most like to be
as we between us do agree
                        or—stir of gramarye
or whatsomever of ferly—who should say?
                        or solid substantiality?
you never know *what* may be
                        —not hereabouts.
No wiseman's son *born* do know
                        not in these whoreson March-lands
of this Welshry.

Yet he sleeps on
                        very deep is his slumber:
how long has he been the sleeping lord?
are the clammy ferns
                        his rustling vallance
does the buried rowan
                        ward him from evil, or
does he ward the tanglewood
                        and the denizens of the wood
are the stunted oaks his gnarled guard
                        or are their knarred limbs
strong with his sap?
Do the small black horses
                        grass on the hunch of his shoulders?

From The Sleeping Lord and other fragments

are the hills his couch
      or is he the couchant hills?
Are the slumbering valleys
      him in slumber
      are the still undulations
the still limbs of him sleeping?
Is the configuration of the land
      the furrowed body of the lord
are the scarred ridges
      his dented greaves
do the trickling gullies
      yet drain his hog-wounds?
Does the land wait the sleeping lord
      or is the wasted land
that very lord who sleeps?

         November 1966 to March 1967

NOTES TO
THE SLEEPING LORD AND OTHER FRAGMENTS

The Tribune's Visitation

GENERAL NOTE

It may be as well to say that 'The Tribune's Visitation' in linked with certain other pieces such as 'The Wall' or 'The Fatigue' in that it is concerned with troops of the Roman garrison in Palestine in the earlier decades of the First Century AD. But while in 'The Fatigue' the date is specific and the men concerned are accidentally involved in the Passion (the date of which is taken as the spring of A.D. 30) in this present piece of the surprise visitation of a Military Tribune to troops of his command it is envisaged as being in any year of those first few decades of the 1st Century. In 'The Fatigue' I take liberties with history in making the troops appear as legionaries and of mixed recruitment in order to evoke the heterogeneous character of the forces of a world imperium.

So in 'The Tribune's Visitation' I make the personnel praetorian troops of the Italica cohort (cf. 'the Italian band' stationed at Caesarea Palaestinae c. A.D. 40 mentioned in Acts X.i) but I again make them of mixed recruitment and again this is for reasons inherent in this present fragment. The 'companion piece' of 'The Tribune's Visitation' might be said to be 'The Tutelar of the Place'.

1. No direct reference is intended here to the mocking of our Lord, but to the widespread annual practices of a saturnalian character at the Hilaria, a festival connected with the goddess Cybele which fell at the Vernal Equinox. The practices could very considerably vary: from primitive cult rites involving the death of a victim to mere horseplay. I suppose the practical jokes of only a little back on our April Fool's Day were a last faint echo of similar equinoctial revels, themselves the echoes of more formidable rites.

2. This stands for *acta diurna*, a daily news bulletin circulated, or publicly displayed, in Rome.

3. This term that survived from the Regular Army and was familiar enough to

From The Sleeping Lord and other fragments

soldiers of the new armies throughout the 1914–18 War, may by now be obsolete. It was used of a brew of tea supposed to be available from the cookhouse for men in barracks or camps in time for 'rouse-parade'.

4. I was thinking of the centurion mentioned in Tacitus' *Annals*, notorious for breaking his vine-stick on the backs of his men and nicknamed by them *Cedo alteram*.

5. The Celtic cult-figure Maponos was equated by Classical writers with Apollo. Lugobelinos is said to be the Celtic form from which Llywelyn derives. The trumpeter 'Taranus' needs some apology. I wrote it by a confusion with Tanarus which occurs on one dedication-stone set up in Roman Chester where it is used as an epithet of Jove, the supreme tutelar of the Roman imperium, the sky-god, Iuppiter Optimus Maximus, whose cult was the official worship of the Roman state and signified the Roman domination on earth. Other figures of the Roman pantheon frequently shared altars with some local tutelar, but in this instance great Jupiter himself is given a barbarian epithet, Tanarus, said to signify the god who roars, and, if so, a Germanic form not dissimilar in meaning from the Roman Tonans, the Thunderer. When writing *The Tribune's Visitation* I had in mind this inscription, but thought it read not Tanaro but Tarano. This was owing to an association with *taran* the Welsh word for thunder. But as, presumably, *taran* derives from some much earlier Celtic form I decided to leave 'Taranus' uncorrected.

6. cf. the traditional air *Of Noble Race was Shenkin* with the 18th(?) Century lines

> 'No more in dear Montgomery
> We drink the dear metheglin'

cymanfa – an assembly; pronounce cum-mán-vah.
The *dd* in *Orddwy* (the land of the Ordovices of central Wales) and the *dd* in *meddlyn* is pronounced as English 'th' in 'then' or 'thou'. The form 'metheglin' is an accepted anglicization.

The Tutelar of the Place

The only notes provided by David Jones for 'The Tutelar of the Place' in *The Sleeping Lord and Other Fragments* are the following glosses on certain Welsh words originally assembled by Vernon Watkins. [Ed.]

brethyn	cloth	*hendref*	ancestral dwelling, winter quarters
bryniau	hills		
caer	fort, castle, city	*pentan*	hob, fire-stone

Notes

tarren	tump, knoll	*troia*	meander, from *troi*, to turn, and Troea, Troy.
tref	hamlet		
trefydd	hamlets		

The Hunt

1. The words *palatini*, Penteulu, *arglwyddi*, and jealousy all rhyme. The word *palasau* (palaces) is pronounced approximately pal-ass-eye, accent on the middle syllable.

    The Penteulu was the term used for the Captain of the Guard of the horse-troop which constituted the *comitatus* of a Welsh ruler. Pronounce pen-tye-lee, accent on the middle syllable.

    Arglwyddi (lords) pronounce approximately arr-gloo-with-ee—stress accent on penultimate syllable. Perhaps arg-glwith-ee conveys it better.

2. This passage in brackets refers to certain incidents and persons (such as Gronw the Radiant) mentioned in the Triads of the Three Faithful War-Bands and the Three Unfaithful War-Bands of the Island of Britain.

3. In the Culhwch narrative mention is made of aid coming from across the Channel, and at Cardigan the hog kills *gwilenhin brenin freinc*. Gwilenhin, King of France.

4. Fferyllt or Fferyll is the Welsh form of the name Vergil. Pronounce approximately, fair-rillt. Owing to the medieval association of Vergil with prophetic and magical powers, any alchemist was called *fferyllt* and later the word became used of any chemist.

5. The term *maer biswail*, 'dung bailiff', was used of the overseer of the villeins who worked on the court farmlands, thus making the jocular distinction between him and the Maer (from Lat. *maior*) of the province, an important executive official.

    The 'shining *matres*, three by three' refers to a possible connection between the female cult-figures sculptured in groups of three of Romano-Celtic Antiquity, called *Deae Matres* and the term *Y Mamau*, The Mothers, used of the fairies in some parts of Wales.

6. Combroges (pronounce com-bro-gees, accent on middle syllable), 'men of the same *patria*' from which word, Cymry, the Welsh people, derives. Compare Allobroges a people of Savoy mentioned by Classical writers and glossed as meaning 'men of a different *patria*'.

7. This passage refers to various complex distinctions listed in the code known as 'The Laws of Hywel Dda'.

From The Sleeping Lord and other fragments

8. The word Arya means the nobles or high-men, and has nothing whatever to do with race. Among the Sumerians, Chinese, Mongols and the Hamitic tribes of Africa, wherever there was a warrior-culture and the cult of the sky-god, the tribal king or chieftain tended to personify that god, and be addressed by the same title. As noted by Mr Christopher Dawson in *The Age of the Gods*, in the case of the Etruscans a whole mixed people are known to history as 'the Lords', merely because their female cult-figure was Turan, The Lady, and their male cult-figure Maristuran, Mars the Lord.

9. The initial letters are in capitals because the reference is not only to a large tract of forest-land but to a district name, Fforest Fawr, an upland area of Breconshire which formed part of the itinerary taken by the boar, Trwyth, and Arthur's hunt.

Note: This fragment is part of an incomplete attempt based on the native Welsh early medieval prose-tale, Culhwch ac Olwen, in which the predominant theme becomes the great hunt across the whole of southern Wales of the boar Trwyth by all the war-bands of the Island led by Arthur.

The Sleeping Lord

1. *ystafell*: chamber. Pronounce us-táv-ell. The word here refers to the private apartment of the lord and his wife within the *llys* or court. It derives from late-Latin *stabellum*, a residence, and in the 9th century stanzas about the destruction of Cynddylan's court the word is used of the whole residence: *Stavell Gyndylan* in the original orthography.

2. Yr Arglwyddes: the wife of the Arglwydd. Pronounce approximately ur ar-glo-óith-ess, 'th' as in breathe.

3. *moelion*: plural of *moel*, a bare hill. Pronounce approximately moil-ee-on.

4. *blaendir*: borderland, but meaning also uplands, high hill-country that is also a place of boundaries. Pronounce approximately blein ('ei' as in height) deerr.

5. *stafell*: see note 1.

6. *taeog*: a villein or man bound to the land. Pronounce approximately tei-og.

7. *ys tywyll heno*: is dark tonight. Pronounce us tuh-will ('ll' represents Welsh *ll*) hen-no, *heb dan*, *heb wely*: without fire, without bed. Pronounce approximately habe dahn, habe wel-ee.

The use here of these two lines requires some explanation seeing that

Notes

my knowledge of Welsh is so extremely scanty and that I have to rely in the main on translations. The lines quoted form part of one of the earliest fragments of Welsh poetry and seem to me to incant and evoke so much that is central to a great tradition at its strongest and most moving. They are part of a ninth-century series of stanzas in which the princess Heledd of Powys laments the death of her brother Cynddylan and the destruction of his court at Pengwern (Shrewsbury) by the Angles. In the older orthography the words of this stanza read

Stavell Gyndylan ys tywyll heno
heb dan, heb wely.

'The "hall" of Cynddylan is dark tonight, without fire without bed.' The words *Stavell Gyndylan* are repeated as the opening words of each of the (sixteen) stanzas so that they burn themselves into the mind, very much as do certain great phrases that echo in a Liturgy, as for example, the words I have ventured to use earlier from the Roman rite of *Tenebrae* 'How does the city sit solitary that was full of people!' Such words, as with these of the princess Heledd have a permanency and evoke a whole situation far beyond their immediate 'meaning' that, in my view, it is our duty to conserve however little we 'know' the original languages.

8. *llannerch*: a glade. Pronounce llan-nerch the 'er' as in errand.

9. *llwyn*: a grove. Pronounce lloo-in.

10. *onnen*: ash tree. Pronounce ón-nen.

11. *coedwig*: a wood. Pronounce coid-wig.

12. *Incedunt arbusta* . . . Perhaps a note is necessary to indicate why I felt impelled to make use of a few words from Ennius, *Annals* Bk. vi, descriptive of the felling by woodmen's axes (*secures*) of the great spreading high trees which he apparently had taken largely from Homer and which Vergil was to use in part from him, and others also, so that the passage has become as it were part of a liturgy whenever the destruction of a woodland is involved. Round about 1936 or 1940 I first heard the Ennius fragment read aloud and the *sound* of the Latin words haunted me and although I could apprehend the meaning only *very* partially and patchily, I *felt* that surely form and content were marvellously wed and a subsequent reading of a translation confirmed my feelings. However, when in 1967 I wished to evoke some part of this passage it was clearly necessary to again consult a translation, and also a friend with a knowledge of Latin which I have not. Further I found it necessary to replace *securibus* by *rapacibus* in that my trees were brought down not 'by axes' but 'by tusks' and similarly *magnas quercus*

From The Sleeping Lord and other fragments

would not do because none of the oaks of the Welsh hill-site I had in mind are by any means 'great' or 'mighty', but, on the contrary, strangling and stunted, so I replaced *magnas* by *sacras* seeing that in so far as one is concerned for and stands within the mythus of this island, the oak, of whatever sort, great or small, has for obvious reasons, sacral associations.

13. Trwyth: pronounce troóith.
14. *ysgithrau*: tusks. Pronounce approximately us-gith-rei.
15. *pentan*: hearth. Pronounce pén-tan.
16. *y twrch dirfawr ysgithrog hir*: the huge hog, long tusked. Pronounce approximately uh toorch deerr-vowrr us-gíth-rog heerr.
17. Ysgyryd: pronounce us-gúh-rid.
18. Mynydd Pen-y-fal: pronounce mun-ith pen-uh-vál; commonly known as 'The Sugar Loaf'. The Welsh name of this mountain means 'the head of the summit'.
19. *caethion*: slaves. Pronounce approximately keith ('ei' as in height) ee-on.
20. Gwendraeth: pronounce approximately gwén-dreith ('ei' as in height).
21. Ystrad Tywi: The Vale of Towy. Pronounce approximately ustrad túh-wee.
22. Gorsedd Arberth: pronounce approximately gorr-seth ('th' as in breathe) árr-berrth ('er' as in errand).
23. *palas*: palace. Pronounce pál-lass.
24. Tawe: pronounce approximately tau-eh.
25. Sirhywi: pronounce approximately seerr-húh-ee.
26. Ebwy: pronounce éb-wee.
27. Taff: pronounce taf, the 'a' is short.
28. Afan: pronounce áv-van.
29. Nedd: pronounce very approximately nathe, as in lathe or bathe.
30. Ogwr: pronounce óg-oorr.
31. Hafren: (Sabrina) pronounce háv-ren.
32. *morben*: headland. Pronounce morr-ben.
33. *yr ogof*: the cave. Pronounce ur óg-ov.

Notes

34. First Antiphon at Matins for the Dead, *Dirige, Domine, Deus meus, in conspectu tuo viam meam*.

35. Burial Service, Roman Rite Antiphon. '*In paradisum deducant te Angeli*', etc.

36. *castell*: castle. Pronounce approximately cáss-tell, 'll' represents the Welsh *ll*.

37. Eingl-Ffrancwyr: Anglo-Frenchmen. Pronounce approximately ain-gl-fránc-weirr.

38. Saeson: Englishmen. Pronounce approximately seis-on.

39. *tir y blaenau*: land of the border uplands. Pronounce approximately teerr uh blein-ei.